£1—

The UFO Report 1992

Other books by Timothy Good

Above Top Secret
Alien Liaison: The Ultimate Secret
The UFO Report 1990
The UFO Report 1991

THE
UFO REPORT
1992

edited by
Timothy Good

SIDGWICK & JACKSON
LONDON

First published in Great Britain in 1991 by Sidgwick & Jackson Limited

Copyright © 1991 by Timothy Good

ISBN 0–283–06107–3 (hardback)
0–283–06108–1 (paperback)

Photoset by Parker Typesetting Service, Leicester
Printed by Mackays of Chatham, Kent
for Sidgwick & Jackson Limited
Cavaye Place
London SW10 9PG

Contents

Editor's Foreword   vii

1   The Evolving Crop Circles   1
    GEORGE WINGFIELD

2   North American Crop Circles in 1990   22
    NORTH AMERICAN INSTITUTE FOR CROP CIRCLE RESEARCH

3   British Official UFO Reports from the 1950s   39
    NICHOLAS REDFERN

4   The Chinese Scene 1990–91   49
    PAUL DONG

5   A Scientific Research Trip to the Soviet Union   58
    RICHARD HAINES

6   The Soviet Scene 1990   64
    NIKOLAI LEBEDEV

7   Gulf Breeze: A Continuing Saga   80
    BOB OECHSLER

8   Puerto Rico's Astounding UFO Situation   99
    JORGE MARTÍN

9   World Round-up of Selected Reports   120
    TIMOTHY GOOD

Appendix   153
  Some UFO Organizations   153
  The Crop Circles   154
  Some UFO Journals   154
  Services   155
  Reporting Sightings   156

Index   157

Editor's Foreword

By all accounts, 1990/91 has yielded yet another rich and varied crop of UFO reports. And whether or not there is a UFO connection, the mystery cropfield formations have proliferated, not just in Great Britain but in other countries, such as the USA and Canada (Chapter 2), USSR, Australia, and Japan.

Of particular significance is the fact that the defence ministries of Belgium and the USSR have now openly acknowledged that unidentified, apparently intelligently-controlled vehicles have intruded into their airspace, have been tracked on radar, and intercepted by air force jets. In Belgium, radar tapes showing one such encounter (30/31 March 1990) were released to the press. On three occasions that night, air force F-16 jets locked on to a target. 'There was a logic in the movements of the UFO,' said Colonel Wilfried De Brouwer, Belgian Air Force Chief of Operations, who ruled out any conventional explanation for the incidents.

Numerous military encounters in the USSR were reported in 1990, including a number of air force interceptions, prompting public commentary by General Igor Maltsev, Chief of Staff of the Air Defence Forces, General Ivan Tretiak, the Soviet Deputy Defence Minister, and even President Mikhail Gorbachev, who admitted that the UFO phenomenon was real and should be treated seriously. Perhaps the most disturbing military case occurred on 13 September 1990, when a large triangular-shaped UFO allegedly landed at a radar complex near Samara, Siberia, and destroyed a radar aerial (Chapter 6).

Among several close encounters reported in China, one of the more impressive incidents took place on 18 March 1991, when an airliner chased a large UFO which divided into two over the Shanghai area (Chapter 4).

The extraordinary series of events reported in Gulf Breeze, Florida, have attracted worldwide attention, but few are aware that the sightings have continued up to the present, and that numerous video films have been taken – some by television company cameramen (Chapter 7).

Puerto Rico, too, has continued to attract a great deal of UFO activity. Many witnesses have observed military aircraft apparently chasing UFOs, and there have been several close encounters, including a sighting of five strange creatures in the Cabo Rojo area and the truly astounding multiple-witness observation of a huge UFO which hovered over an electricity substation in the town of Trujillo Alto on 17 March 1991, causing $355,000 in damage costs (Chapter 8).

Sadly, it remains an uphill struggle to persuade the media to take a serious interest in these important matters. In a recent commentary in the *Sunday Telegraph*[1] on my book, *Alien Liaison: The Ultimate Secret* (Century 1991), for example, Michael Harrington chose to ridicule all those who believe in UFOs, including Admiral Lord Hill-Norton and several other distinguished former public servants, carefully avoiding any mention of the abundance of sightings by highly qualified observers such as military and civilian pilots (now said to number well over 3,000), or the overwhelming evidence of extensive monitoring of the phenomenon by the military and intelligence community.

When such articles appear in the press, I encourage people to write to the editors of the newspapers concerned. In a letter to the *Sunday Telegraph*, my friend Graham Sheppard, a British Airways captain, described one of his sightings as follows:

'Some years ago I saw a UFO flying in controlled airspace over Central England. We were alerted to its approach by the Preston Radar controller who advised us that "fast-moving opposite direction traffic is in your 12 o'clock, height unknown". Within seconds, an archetypal metallic disc, a little smaller than a Trident airliner, appeared and flew past us very fast and not more than a quarter of a mile away ... All three of us on the flight deck of the Vanguard saw the UFO. We were in no way mistaken.

'Twenty years on, our reasoning for not formally reporting the sighting is well supported in the chillingly dismissive article by Michael Harrington ... Believe me when I say that I would much prefer the whole manifestation to be as fanciful as suggested. However, there is no doubt for me that someone with highly advanced technology is casually and continuously using the airspace of our planet ... Even at this stage it is not easy to disclose my position or the airline for which I have flown for twenty-five years, but time has passed and I feel it essential that qualified and experienced observers such as myself should stand up to be counted ...'[2]

Graham Sheppard is to be commended for his courage. This

particular letter was not published, but I feel that if a sufficient number of people keep writing to newspaper editors each time similar articles appear, we could begin to see a more positive attitude to this controversial subject. In addition, I urge all those impressed by the evidence for UFOs to write to their Member of Parliament or other representatives.

1990 has seen the passing of two fine UFO researcher/writers. Sometime between 14–16 August, D. Scott Rogo was stabbed to death at his home in Northridge near Los Angeles[3]. Born in 1950, Scott gained a BA in the psychology of music from California State University and played the oboe with a number of symphony orchestras. His books include *The Haunted Universe* and *The Tujunga Canyon Contacts* (co-authored with Ann Druffel). He edited *UFO Abductions* and wrote many articles on parapsychology for various magazines, including a monthly column for *Fate*. I met Scott Rogo only once, and was impressed by his cheerful and intelligent approach to the UFO phenomenon.

John Fuller, playwright, documentary film producer, and author of many books about the unexplained, died at the age of 76 on 7 November 1990. In addition to two Broadway plays, Fuller was best-known for his books on UFOs and the paranormal, including *The Ghost of Flight 401*, *The Interrupted Journey*, *Incident at Exeter*, and *Aliens in the Skies*.[4]

Sadly, I have to report that a photograph published in *The UFO Report 1991* now appears to have been faked. Peter Woolaway, who took the photograph of an alleged UFO on 27 February 1990 at Bartley Green Reservoir, Birmingham, has not given me satisfactory answers to certain technical questions (relating to the focal length of the lens used and the size of the 'UFO') and avoided an opportunity for a personal discussion with me.

I am happy to report that a major documentary on UFOs is in the preproduction stage. Based on material contained in my books and provisionally entitled *Above Top Secret*, the Anglo–American documentary is scheduled for transmission in late 1992 or early 1993.

Together with a number of researchers, I have been cooperating with a US Senate enquiry into the misappropriation of huge sums of money in Government 'black budget' UFO studies, and hope to report on any results in the future. In addition, I am hoping to obtain confirmation for the allegations made by Bob Oechsler regarding the 'Cosmic Journey' project (described in *Alien Liaison*). In June 1991, during a trip to Washington DC., I visited the Old Executive Office Building adjoining the White House and briefly discussed the matter with a former astronaut who works with the National Space Council. To my regret, I learned nothing, but was promised to be kept informed.

I would like to take this opportunity to reaffirm my support for Bob Oechsler. Predictably, there have been attempts to discredit him, particularly relating to his claim that the United States has acquired a number of extraterrestrial spacecraft, as apparently confirmed by former National Security Agency director Admiral Inman, and Rear Admiral Shapiro, a former director of Naval Intelligence, and a general at the Pentagon. These gentlemen have now denied confirming anything of the sort. Yet we have a tape recording of Bob's conversation with Admiral Inman, as well as a recording of a warning by Inman's executive assistant that any public disclosure of the information acquired would violate national secrecy laws.

At a conference in Tucson, Arizona, in May 1991, Robert Dean, a retired US Army command sergeant-major, claimed that NATO's Supreme Headquarters Allied Powers Europe (SHAPE) conducted a highly secret investigation into UFOs from 1961–64. Dean, who held a Cosmic Top Secret clearance at the time, claims to have read an 8-inch thick document (consisting mostly of annexes), which became known as 'The Assessment'. The study allegedly concluded that the Earth was under extensive surveillance by several advanced extraterrestrial civilizations. Robert Dean has supplied further details, including names of those involved, and I am cooperating with him in an endeavour to provide corroboration.

Finally, I am indebted to the team of dedicated contributors who have made this book possible, and to the numerous journalists, researchers, magazines and newspapers whose reports are cited herein. My apologies for any omissions of credit.

TIMOTHY GOOD
London
July 1991

REFERENCES
1. Harrington, Michael: 'Why Credulity Springs Eternal', *Sunday Telegraph*, London, 7 July 1991.
2. Letter from Graham Sheppard to the Editor of the *Sunday Telegraph*, 9 July 1991.
3. *MUFON UFO Journal*, No. 269, September 1990.
4. Obituary by Edwin McDowell, *New York Times*, 9 November 1990.

1

The Evolving Crop Circles

GEORGE WINGFIELD

Educated at Eton College and Trinity College, Dublin, George Wingfield graduated in 1966 with an MA Hons. degree in Natural Sciences. He worked briefly at the Royal Greenwich Observatory, Herstmonceux, on stellar spectra and the Earth's magnetism, and currently works for IBM UK Ltd in the field of Systems Engineering.

George Wingfield became interested in the Cropfield Circles phenomenon on 8 August 1987, after visiting Westbury, Wiltshire, where a number of circle formations had recently appeared. This also led to an interest in the related subject of Ufology. Widely recognized as a leading authority, he is a Director of Field Research for the Centre for Crop Circle Studies (CCCS), and has lectured on this intriguing phenomenon throughout the UK and USA.

The English Crop Circles in 1990 developed and evolved in ways which few people could ever have imagined. The year marked a quantum leap in their evolution with the development of 'pictograms', and the total number of Circle events recorded was far higher than the previous year's total; most probably well in excess of 1,000.

Unprecedented new shapes such as 'dumb-bells', rectangles, triangles, 'scrolls' and semi-circular rings were found. The size of some individual Circles also far exceeded what had been recorded before. But most staggering of all was the appearance of the pictograms: elaborate formations of up to 150 yards long, whose complexity and varying combinations of certain distinctive features exhibited an articulateness which the Circles had never previously shown.

This rapid growth in the complexity of the Circles during 1990 was so marked that none but the most hardened self-deluding sceptic could possibly seek to deny it. It is an aspect which had been clearly apparent in earlier years, but one which accelerated with seemingly increased urgency in 1990. Theories which claim to explain the Circles cannot afford to ignore this unmistakable evolution, however unwelcome it

1

may be to those whose fixed ideas have failed to appreciate the real nature of this phenomenon. Nevertheless, it is true to say that an explanation of what is happening – in terms generally acceptable and understood – seemed as remote as ever in 1990 and 1991. But the idea that some intelligence is at work has gained considerable ground, though it is still not possible to say whether this is physical or non-physical, from this Earth or from without, or even whether it is linked with or in some way reflects the collective consciousness of humanity.

Wiltshire's Giant Ringed Circles

The first 1990 Circles started in late April and early May, to the north of Devizes. In addition to a plethora of small Circles, several large ringed Circles appeared in the young crops. All of these exhibited very precise narrow rings, usually 6–9 inches wide, of a variety not seen in earlier years. The first ever triple-ringed Circle had appeared in late 1989; now we had two more of these near Devizes, one with four small satellites on the second ring. These giants were all accompanied by 'grapeshot'.

The largest of the giant triple-ringed Circles was one which I discovered during an aerial survey to have 'grown' an extra outer (fourth) concentric ring one week after it first formed. A few days later, on 1 June, another giant Circle with four concentric rings, and with four satellites on its second ring, appeared less than a mile away. This reinforced the idea, often expressed by dowsers of the Circles such as Richard Andrews, that the prevailing configuration of the energy field at the time of formation, which is detectable by dowsing, determines the actual pattern of the resulting Circle. Immediately adjacent to this prodigy, a new 'Celtic Cross', with four satellites on its widely spaced single ring, appeared on 5 July. One satellite was neatly positioned at one of the two points where this orbital ring intersected the outer ring of the older formation.

On 18 May, the first Cheesefoot Head (Hampshire) Circle of 1990 appeared in the Punchbowl there, as has become almost traditional. This was unlike other Circles in having an internal concentric band of standing corn. There soon followed other Circles, such as two triple-ringers (with wide rings, each about 4 feet thick, quite unlike the Wiltshire ones), one having the inner rings in the form of segmented arcs, which had never previously been seen. But at the same time, even curiouser geometric patterns were starting to appear nearby. On 23 May, the first of the pictogram series of Circle formations was found between Chilcomb and Cheesefoot Head.

The Pictograms

The basic component of these formations is a 'dumb-bell' consisting of two Circles joined by a straight avenue of flattened crop, as can be seen in the photographs (Plates 1.4/7). The first one also had the feature of two narrow parallel rectangles on either side of its avenue, and these were often repeated, in pairs or singly, in subsequent pictograms. Other features, such as semicircular rings concentric with one Circle, followed, and many of the series had one or other of the dumb-bell Circles ringed. These pictograms constituted an extraordinary development in the Circle saga, and again and again cereologists [those who study the phenomenon – Ed.] shook their heads in disbelief as they repeated the familiar litany for 1990: 'Never seen anything like this before . . .'

Roughly every week or so, a further pictogram appeared near Cheesefoot Head (with one at Litchfield – an old Circles site 17 miles north, unvisited since 1985) until Pictogram No. 7 on 6 July. Many of these incorporated a tractor tramline as the dumb-bell's shaft, making it into part of the design. This unmistakable characteristic, though not invariably present, confirmed a frequent tendency of many Circle formations (such as quincunxes in previous years) to align themselves with the tramlines, though this was questioned by some observers. The fact that the agency which causes the formations is 'aware' of the tramlines, and makes use of them, must cast serious doubt on the notion that the Circles-forming agency descends randomly from the sky.

The Wansdyke Watch

In June, John Haddington organized a Circles watch lasting ten days, between Silbury Hill and Wansdyke. During this, the 'trilling' noise (referred to in the 1991 *UFO Report*) was heard again by several people, and other strange noises, including a 'swishing' sound, were heard in fields where Circles subsequently formed. John and a companion also watched on one occasion a yellow luminous object low over one of these fields, and several smaller red lights which seemed to come out of the larger object.

This area near Silbury Hill seems especially prone to such sightings, which are highly reminiscent of the Warminster UFO flap of the 1960s and 1970s. Again and again, one is left with the impression that one's ordinary five senses have been somehow inadequate in their perception of the event witnessed. There is an unmistakable impression that whatever was observed was in some way controlled and not of a natural or random nature; but what these things are remains a total mystery.

I myself observed mysterious lights in this area during and after the Wansdyke Watch. These were very small and faint and moved slowly and deliberately close to the heads of the wheat, at a distance of perhaps 200–300 yards from us. At first I thought that this was no more than a trick of the light in conditions of low visibility. But on another occasion, together with John and another observer, I watched these tiny lights for more than an hour from a Circle formation near Milk Hill, just south of Wansdyke. The lights would move about, fade, gather, sometimes brighten and then usually fade away altogether. It was not possible to approach them, and if one tried to do so they would just fade away.

Certainly these were not glow-worms (with which I am familiar) or fireflies – or, for that matter, swamp gas, which some people might suggest. Perhaps they were the elusive 'Will o'the Wisp' of old . . . But what I do know is that in each of the fields where we saw these lights, small grapeshot Circles appeared at a later date.

To increase the chances of seeing a Circle form, the Wansdyke Watch group consulted medium Isabelle Kingston, who claims to have received many 'channelled' communications relating to the Circles. After some mapdowsing, she recommended that the fields below the great tumulus Adam's Grave, near Alton Barnes, be watched, since she said that Circles would form just there. It was not a place where Circles had formed previously and was nearly 2 miles from the nearest of last year's Circles. This was the only place which Isabelle specified. As a result, several nights were spent by the group watching from Adam's Grave for Circles; but none appeared during the course of our vigil.

The Alton Barnes Pictogram

A month later, on 12 July, the most remarkable, and what was to become the best known ever, set of Circles appeared in the wheatfield below Adam's Grave at Alton Barnes. This spectacular giant pictogram, the eighth to form, consisted basically of two dumb-bell formations together in line, with several additional Circles, the whole extending over about 130 yards. The major Circles in the dumb-bells, either ringed or plain, were all swept clockwise (as with Hampshire pictograms), but these exhibited protruding features never previously seen. Variously referred to as 'keys' and 'claws', they resembled rudimentary hands with either two or three 'fingers'.

At the same time, a further similar giant pictogram was discovered near Milk Hill, close by. This too had 'keys' or 'claws' protruding from the principal Circles. Both giant pictograms pointed directly away from the Alton Barnes White Horse, carved in chalk on the slopes of Milk

Hill, and both lay approximately three-quarters of a mile from it. It is surely no coincidence that the White Horse, for which the Circles have always shown a marked predilection, as at Westbury and Cherhill in particular, symbolizes the gateway between the physical world and the psychic, or metaphysical, domain.

A villager in Alton Barnes, half a mile away, had heard a strange humming noise from East Field on the night before the great pictogram was found there, and several of the village dogs had started barking. Other stories told of cars in the village which would not start that morning. The beauty and mystery of this mysterious labyrinth which had appeared in East Field drew people like a magnet.

Many people travelled from all over the country to Alton Barnes during the next month to see this new wonder of the world. Their sense of excitement and awe was often quite palpable to others who were there, and few of them doubted that this was some intelligently produced, but obscure, symbolic message. Many of these visitors seemed deeply affected by what they found, and some observed that this pilgrimage had all the makings of a new religion. Farmer Tim Carson wisely cashed in on this fervour and curiosity by charging £1 admission to the field, thereby netting over £5,000.

The Milk Hill UFO

Two miles away from the Alton Barnes pictogram, another very similar formation had appeared the same night on farmer David Read's land. This was less known and less visited, although equally remarkable. It was also the venue of a daytime UFO sighting which was recorded on video by two visitors to the pictogram on 26 July.

This couple had walked over Milk Hill to look at the pictogram and were returning up over the hill. A final glance at the great double-dumb-bell caused them to catch sight of a small white object low over the wheat in the field below. On the 4 minutes of videotape that they recorded, this object is seen to emit a pulsating light. It moves purposively over the wheatfield, pausing occasionally, and at one time going down into the crop before re-emerging from a tramline gap. The object is seen to part the wheat as it moves into it. Finally, it flies up into the sky, passing over the head of a tractor driver before disappearing in the distance.

This extraordinary piece of film was shown to Colin Andrews, who later returned to Alton Barnes and Stanton St Bernard to look for the tractor driver. This was some weeks after the UFO incident had occurred. Leon, the tractor driver had initially told people that he had seen a tiny disc fly over him and, as can be imagined, had received nothing but ridicule and knowing looks from most people who, naturally, thought they knew better. As in other UFO cases, it was not long before he learned to keep the matter very much to himself.

When Colin produced the videotape, quite clearly showing the tractor and driver besides this mysterious object, Leon, unlike the vast majority of single witnesses to UFO events, found himself completely vindicated. Sceptics have attempted to convince us that the object was a plastic bag blown by the wind, or else that the British Army had a new line in highly sophisticated remotely piloted vehicles (RPVs). Neither explanation will do. This was indeed a UFO in the fullest sense of that acronym, though we have no idea of its origin or purpose.

[Editor's note: Thanks to the BBC TV 'Cropwatch' team, I have studied this remarkable video film very carefully, and can report that the object shown is not a bird, a kite, a balloon, a plastic bag, or an RPV; at least, it's not one of *our* RPVs!]

Operation Blackbird

In view of the massive press coverage of the pictograms (at Alton Barnes in particular), there is no doubt that the Government was fully aware of, if not alarmed by, public reaction to these events. The Army was seen to take a great interest in the new Circles, and much activity, especially with helicopters, was observed in the Silbury Hill area in the following weeks. The military also became closely involved with Colin Andrews and Pat Delgado's 'Operation Blackbird' Circles watch at Bratton, which ran for three weeks from 23 July. Sponsored by BBC TV and Nippon TV, this was a hi-tech attempt, like the previous year's Project White Crow, to film a Circle forming. At times, however, it risked turning into a media circus.

On 25 July, amid fanfares of media hype, the Blackbird team announced via the BBC that they had video-recorded 'a major event' – flashing orange lights in the sky above a field where a large new formation of Circles had appeared during the night. But within a few hours, the crowning glory of success crumbled into dust when it was found that the roughly fashioned six Circles were no more than an elaborate hoax, and that the unknown deceivers had left a game and a wooden cross at the dead centre of each.

6

A Carefully Planned Hoax

COLIN ANDREWS: Well, we do have a major event here ... er, very much excitement, as you can imagine. We do have two major ground markings ... have appeared in front of all of the surveillance equipment, performing absolutely to form for us. We had a situation at approximately 3.30 a.m. this morning. On the monitor a number of orange lights taking the form of a triangle ... it's a complex situation, and we are actually analysing it at this very moment, but there is undoubtedly something here for science.

NICHOLAS WITCHELL *(BBC newsreader):* I'm sure you have the nation agog. Are you quite sure you couldn't have been the victims of some elaborate hoax last night?

COLIN ANDREWS: No, not indeed ... we have high-quality equipment here and we have indeed secured on high-quality equipment a major event ... We do have something of great, great significance ... Yes, we have everything on film and we do have, as I say, a formed object over the field ... We are doing nothing more now until we have helicopters over the top, to film in detail what we have, before anyone enters the field.

To those of us listening to the early news on 25 July, the excitement in Colin Andrews' voice left little room for doubt that Operation Blackbird had turned up trumps and that, at last, the formation of a whole array of Crop Circles had been recorded on videotape. Here finally was proof that the Circles were produced by some mysterious and elusive agency, possibly related to UFOs, and that they were definitely not the work of hoaxers, though this view was no longer widespread after the amazing 1990 pictograms.

But Andrews' and Delgado's apparent triumph was, alas, short-lived. When they did go down into the new Circles that morning, they saw immediately evidence of human involvement. At the dead centre of each of the six circles had been placed a 'Horoscope' board-game (subsequently incorrectly described as an ouija board) and a rough wooden cross. There was also a piece of red wire whose length corresponded to the diameter of some of the six Circles. The wheat was in places trampled and broken, and it was not flattened to the ground with quite the same smooth regularity and sheen which we had seen so often in the 1990 pictograms.

The palpable embarrassment of the BBC in its later admission that this was a hoax, and the anger that was felt at Blackbird that morning was nothing compared to the disappointment of Circles watchers everywhere and those who had been gripped by the subject. We all felt desperately sorry for Colin Andrews, whose credibility had been severely damaged, and angry that serious Circles research had been

7

subjected to ridicule by this cruel hoax. Colin's initial statements were undoubtedly ill-advised, perhaps even unwise in the extreme. But this had been predictable, since Blackbird had been turned into a media circus, and he was under great pressure to 'deliver the goods'.

The surveillance project was said to be using hi-tech equipment valued at £1 million. This included several video-recording systems, infra-red cameras and image intensifiers, which should have revealed anything which moved in the dark out in those fields to the north of Bratton Castle (an ancient Iron Age hill-fort). Here, on the edge of an escarpment, was perched the Blackbird observation post, a large portakabin housing the much-vaunted surveillance kit. Only hours before the hoax was perpetrated, I had been told that 'only a rabbit has to move between here and Trowbridge [four miles away] for us to know all about it'.

Sadly, the truth was very different. The range of the infra-red equipment was very limited, providing images of dubious quality at over 600 yards. During much of the project, the availability of the equipment fell well below 100 per cent because there was no engineer continuously on site to maintain it. And at those critical times when things were actually happening in the fields below – both at the time of the hoax and when a real set of Circles appeared later – the duty crew either failed to notice anything on their screens at the time, or else were asleep.

The Army, who apparently own the land on which the observation post was situated, were deeply involved in Blackbird. They were most helpful and encouraging, and supplied men to help with the surveillance. The soldiers at Blackbird, though officially off-duty, did not wear civilian clothes. The Army also carried out considerable additional night surveillance of its own, using night-sights and the like, which gave far clearer vision of the fields being watched than anything in the observation post. This equipment was manned by soldiers with blackened faces hiding in camouflaged dens.

Rather curiously, the two corporals assigned for duty at the Blackbird observation post were absent on the night of the hoax, though they were there on every other night of the project. Corporal Darren Cummings was reported to have told the press: 'We are here to prove that they [the Circles] are caused by people; the scientists are here to prove otherwise.'

In retrospect, there can be no doubt that Andrews and Delgado were set up. This was no spur-of-the-moment hoax done by jolly young farmers after a night's drinking in The Oak at Westbury or The Duke at Bratton. Nor, clearly, was it the work of one man. All the hallmarks of a very carefully prepared deception could be seen. Whatever was said about the hoaxed formation in farmer Jonathan King's field being crudely trampled, like several other hoaxed Circles made later, this array of six Circles and parallel lines was brilliantly executed. In fact, as man-made Circles go, these were as good as one might ever hope to achieve.

One group, consisting of a triple-ringed Circle with two small satellites, closely resembled a formation which had appeared near Cheesefoot Head on 30 May. Beyond that, a triple-in-line with a large ringed central Circle was curiously similar to a formation which had appeared beside the Warminster bypass a few weeks earlier. Between the two groups lay three not very straight parallel lines, at right angles to the tramlines and unlike anything seen previously. Viewed from an aeroplane, the geometry can be seen to be somewhat imperfect and unlike genuine Circles. However, this was certainly not apparent when viewed at a shallow oblique angle, as it was from the Blackbird observation post. Most telling of all is the fact that this formation exhibited no dowsable pattern, as genuine Circles do.

An Attempt to Shift the Blame?

Quite evidently, the Circles had been faked with great care and their creator had gone to great lengths to produce a superficially convincing formation which initially deceived all of the Blackbird observers. Then why were the strange artefacts, the Horoscope game-board and the wooden crosses left behind in the circles? This simply did not make sense. If a hoaxer wished to achieve a masterly deception, he would not then deliberately give the game away with these obvious signs that the Circles were man-made.

In reporting the hoax, the BBC said that the objects suggested some kind of a ritual. Surely nothing could be further from the truth: no ritualist would conceivably perform under such circumstances, in front of a massive surveillance operation. The only explanation was that the hoaxers wanted to pin the blame on New Age or occult groups, which the naïve might believe were associated with supposedly ritualistic objects.

Among those on the Blackbird watch there was the definite impression that not only had Andrews and Delgado been set up, but that this was an inside job. The hoaxers seemed to have known that, at half a mile's distance, they were just out of the effective range of the image intensifying equipment. They seemed aware that Andrews and Delgado were not present on the night of the hoax, and that the Army corporals were also absent. It also seemed that they knew of the previously agreed procedure, which stipulated that no one should enter any Circles that formed during the watch until they had first been surveyed from the air.

Most telling of all was that the hoaxers seemed to have correctly anticipated Colin Andrews' reactions and what he might say to the media before the Circles had been thoroughly examined. This hoax was clearly thought out with the greatest precision, and executed when the time was right, which happened to be on just the second night of the project. And who, after all, would happen to have six Horoscope game-boards on hand unless it had all been well prepared in advance?

So who were the cunning perpetrators of this odd deception and, more importantly, what were their motives? There was no shortage of candidates. On the day after the hoax, Colin Andrews received a letter, postmarked Nottingham, which seemed to have been sent by the pop group KLF (Kopyright Liberation Front), a.k.a. The Timelords. It read:

> Colin, the circles on Wednesday were just a hoax, but we can't help to play jokes. Inconvenience caused? We're sorry. Catch us, you'll have to hurry. Yours, in total control, the Justified Ancients of Mu Mu – the Jamms. Try not to worry too hard. We find it very funny while you sit back and rake in the money.

At the bottom of the page was drawn the KLF's logo, a pyramid crossed by a long ghettoblaster, then the numbers 25 and 31 and the word Wiltshire. The letter had been posted on 25 July, the day the Circles appeared.

For those of you who are not into Acid House music and the like, these references may seem incomprehensible. The KLF, consists of Bill Drummond and Jimmy Cauti, alias The JAMMs, and they were best known for their number one hit, 'Doctorin' the Tardis', with rock star Gary Glitter. It was thought that the hoax might have been intended to publicize their new album, *Space*.

Listeners to Forces Request programmes will know that the KLF and Acid House numbers are popular with the 'squaddies'. The '25' presumably referred to the date of the hoax, 25 July, and the '31' may have been the intended date for a further hoax circle. A mystery man with a long straggly beard, wearing a lady's blue suede coat, a skirt and a bowler hat, who was seen on White Horse Hill near the Blackbird observation post earlier on the night of the hoax, was thought to have been Bill Drummond.

At the time, Colin Andrews and Pat Delgado accepted that this pop group were most likely the ones who hoaxed the circles. This seemed to be confirmed a week later on 2 August, when a further hoaxed circle was seen in the fields between Silbury Hill and Wansdyke. This vast design, 80 yards across, was an unmistakable representation of the

KLF's logo – the pyramid and ghettoblaster. Here again, Richard Andrews and Busty Taylor soon proved by dowsing that this was not a genuine Circle. Others unfamiliar with KLF and still reeling from the extraordinary developments of the 1990 pictograms were prepared to accept it as real.

I sought out farmer David Read, on whose land this lay, and asked what he made of it. He told me that he had been approached by four people who wanted to make their own crop Circle. They would pay for the damage caused, if he would show them where to make it, and let them create what they said was a work of art. He took them to a field with a comparatively poor crop of wheat, and left them to work on it.

The KLF logo Circle took nearly 6 hours to complete, using yard-brush broomhandles, planks, lengths of cord and marker poles. The two members of the band, the wife of one of them, and film-maker Bill Butt came away exhausted and with badly blistered hands, just as it was getting dark. Pleased with their work, they filmed it from the air the next day, and this Circle, which they insist was not a hoax but landscape art, is featured, together with the black rapper who does the vocals, in Bill's promotional video for their latest number, 'What Time is Love?'

I have spoken at length with Bill Butt and he assures me that the band did not send the JAMMs letter to Colin Andrews. Neither were they responsible for the Bratton hoax. On this, they are quite adamant and there is every reason to believe them. Although they had fostered a myth in the rock music world that they had been 'circling' for years, their first attempt at a crop Circle resulted in a 'pathetic little mess in the corner of the field'. They then determined to do something like the Bratton hoax.

Bill Butt flew a hired microlight near Silbury Hill looking for a suitable venue. Having selected possible places he then went to negotiate for a field with David Read, and paid him £350 to make the Circle. Few people knew of their intention at this time and it still had not been decided to make their Circle like the KLF logo. Their 'prom video' did not feature any real Circles, just the logo one.

The curious business of the letter showing the logo remains unsolved. There is no certainty that this was sent by the Bratton hoaxers, though it is a distinct possibility. But the fact that the logo Circle took KLF so long to make, and the fact they paid the farmer for the privilege, hardly squares up with the expertly made Bratton hoax, created in perhaps one hour in total darkness.

Among other contenders for the dubious distinction of having made the hoax is George Vernon of Bristol, a.k.a. Merlin the Magician. (I am not inventing these people, even though some of them sound to be pure

11

fantasy, or at any rate candidates for Lord Sutch's Monster Raving Loony Party.) Merlin, it is said, markets the Horoscope zodiacal tell-your-fortune game. He also claims to be responsible for making all the Crop Circles through the power of his mind. This faculty he discovered some years ago when he slept in a cornfield near Stonehenge and awoke to find a Circle had formed around him. Next year he intends to produce Circles in the state of Illinois, USA.

For reasons best known to himself, Merlin says he faked the Bratton Circles by rolling around in the corn, since his mental powers had evidently forsaken him that night. This story was told by a fearless reporter from the *Sunday Sport*, Bertie Ollocks. And if you believe what you read in the *Sunday Sport*, let alone something written by a man called B. Ollocks, then I dare say you'll believe anything.

Some Military Intelligence

A week after the Bratton hoax, I was still wrestling with the inconsistencies of this baffling puzzle, and the illogicality of the boards and crosses in particular. It was then that I received a call from a friend which put an entirely new complexion on the matter. He has a reliable contact in a senior position in the military, whose name cannot be disclosed for obvious reasons. This man had supplied sensitive information in the past which had always proved to be good. He now revealed that the Bratton hoax had been carried out by a specially set-up detachment of the Army and had been ordered from a high level in the Ministry of Defence. The operation had been carefully planned, practised in advance and then executed swiftly and precisely in total darkness at short notice. Our source had even spoken to an officer involved in the planning of the operation, which was carried out in the utmost secrecy.

If this information proves to be untrue, I shall be the first to withdraw the allegation. But his solution is the only one that explains the many puzzling aspects of the case. To understand the motive, one has to appreciate the extraordinary situation which had arisen at the end of July. With the advent of the pictograms and the giant formation at Alton Barnes in particular, Circles hysteria had risen almost to fever-pitch. The newspapers were full of Circles, and people were driving from all over the country to Wiltshire and Hampshire to see the phenomena. The excitement and exhilaration among those who come to Alton Barnes was quite palpable. Yet the Government said nothing, did nothing and was probably as perplexed as almost everybody else.

Somehow the situation had to be defused, and the best way of doing this was to make the populace believe that the Circles were no more than elaborate hoaxes. To do this, an elaborate hoax had to be executed, which appeared the equal of the real phenomenon, and yet could be seen to be a hoax. Blackbird would present the perfect opportunity. Thus the plot was hatched, and it was called into play on only the second night of the project, when Andrews and Delgado were not on the scene.

But why the Horoscope boards and wooden crosses? To achieve its objective, the hoax had to be seen to be a hoax. There was always the ghastly possibility that Andrews and Delgado might proclaim the hoaxed Circles as genuine, thereby defeating the purpose of the whole exercise, and redoubling public fervour for the Circles. Therefore, these artefacts were placed, with tell-tale military precision, at the centre of each Circle, the items having being chosen to implicate a very different group of people from those actually concerned.

If we had listened to Corporal Cummings (though I do not say he was a party to this deception) we might have understood what lay behind the Bratton hoax. As it was, the operation was a complete success, for within days the newspapers were vying with each other to run articles ridiculing the Circles and to prove that they were indeed all hoaxes. Nevertheless, the Army presence at Bratton and around Silbury Hill, and at Beckhampton, continued unabated for three more weeks, with extreme interest being shown in genuine Circle formations. The Army had indeed 'proved' that the circles were made by people, although it knew full well that this was not the truth of the matter.

Operation Blackbird did eventually video-record the forming of a genuine set of crop Circles – the 'Question Mark' – produced without any human involvement. But the organisers and sponsors of Blackbird, 'once bitten twice shy', made no public announcement of this coup whatever. It seems that this piece of film, because of its poor quality, will not be shown by the BBC in the near future, despite the small fortune that was spent by them in obtaining it.

There is little doubt that the Government is embarrassed by the Circles situation and seriously worried about what action to take this year when strange events start happening in the cornfields once more. Evidence of this is demonstrated by a claim that a secret ministerial meeting was called in September 1990 to discuss the subject. No doubt they were very well briefed by the military, but it was allegedly stated at this meeting that the cause of the Circles was completely unknown.

The chief concern of those present was that the Government should not be placed in the embarrassing position of having to admit to its ignorance, and with this in mind the subject of disinformation was raised several times. For the present, the military was left with a watching brief and no doubt we will see more of them in the field this summer.

Aftermath of the Hoax

To some extent, the operation had the desired result, and the Sunday papers were soon all clamouring that all the circles were hoaxes. *The Mail on Sunday* irresponsibly carried instructions on how to make one's own Circle, and another tabloid produced Fred Day (59), who had been making Circles for forty-seven years. There, at last, the mystery was solved and they laid claim to the £10,000 offered by another paper for a solution! Such facile reasoning demonstrated little else than the idiocy of certain journalists.

Meanwhile, the genuine Circles continued to form. On the same day as the Bratton hoax, an extraordinary set of new Circles appeared near Beckhampton, 15 miles away. These included 'scrolls' – circles joined by a sinuous flattened path like a reversed 'S' – and the first reported triangles. All were strongly dowsable. The Army showed much interest in these, photographing them from a small unmanned helicopter known as a WISP. This it had omitted to do at the Bratton hoax site, for obvious reasons.

More pictograms were to follow the amazing Alton Barnes formation. On 27 July, a similar but even larger double dumb-bell pictogram, 150 yards long, was found one mile from Silbury Hill, from which it pointed away almost exactly. This was placed precisely half way between West and East Kennett Long Barrows, and, unlike the other giant picto-grams, lay athwart the tractor tramlines. Despite several hoaxed Circles which various jokers were now producing, there is no suggestion that this or any of the other pictograms was a hoax. Indeed, farmer David Read, on whose land this huge formation lay, said at a later date that he was now totally sure that these formations were not man-made, since he had seen the effort involved in faking much less complex Circles such as that made by the KLF band (not to mention that the faked Circle looked entirely different from the genuine article).

And in the end, Operation Blackbird did catch a real Circle forming, very rapidly, on its video-recording equipment, as I commented earlier. Unfortunately, this was at the extreme limit of the infra-red camera's range and no detail can be discerned, but it proves that a Circle forms very rapidly, with no human intervention. This formation was almost in the shape of a very large question mark, and, in the considered opinion of many of us familiar with this strange phenomenon, there is little doubt that this is just what it was meant to be.

On 4 August 1990, a great new pictogram appeared at Cheesefoot Head, scarcely 40 yards from the second pictogram which had arrived two months earlier. Three times as long, this extraordinary cipher included a wide ring enclosing two long rectangular parallel 'boxes' on either side of its main 'avenue'. This striking feature had appeared earlier in a less elaborate pictogram near Pepperbox Hill outside Salisbury. Three other plain circles and four arcs, symmetrically disposed along the main axis, completed the design. There was 'tremendous energy throughout this configuration', according to Lucy Pringle, a psychic, and this was independently confirmed by George de Trafford and Janet Trevisan, who perceived a 'domed disc of energy' about 12 feet off the ground above the middle Circle.

From June, CCCS received scattered reports of Circles from all over England and some from Scotland. Many were from places where Circles had never previously been found and sometimes they were of formations not previously known, such as a Circle with seven satellites at Bickington, Devon. This was found the day after a large bullet-shaped UFO, with a line of coloured lights flashing in sequence below it, had been seen travelling slowly and silently over Bickington towards Haytor. Also, a set of Circles was found for the first time near the ancient henge of Wandlebury near Cambridge. Like the first Circles near Silbury Hill in 1988, these were positioned on the 'Mary current', a line of dowsable energy which runs right across England and is described in the book *The Sun and the Serpent* by Hamish Miller and Paul Broadhurst (Pendragon Press, 1989).

Further Circles and a Few UFO Reports

In July and August, pictogram formations were found near Salisbury and in Sussex, and a curious triangular formation of Circles joined by flattened pathways except on one side was found near Duns in Scotland. This, like many Circles, appeared close to an ancient burial mound which stood just 70 feet away. Large numbers of Circles were reported from the north of England, notably near Wigan, Lancashire. And at least forty Circles were reported in Norfolk, not previously known for the phenomenon.

Some of the Norfolk circles were accompanied by UFO reports (see Appendix). That which appeared near Swafield, on 26 July, was preceded by the sighting on the previous night of an orange light which went down near where the Circle was subsequently found. A strange formation of Circles at Hopton, consisting of a ringed Circle with ten satellites spaced around it, was found in the place where a great red light the size of a full moon was observed descending into a field on the night of 30 July. The object was said to have had a Saturn-like ring around it, and blinked out on reaching the ground. Several people saw this and it was reported to the police. The actual position of the circles is again on, or extremely close to, the 'Mary current' line through Hopton.

As the 1990 Circle season drew to a close with the August harvest, reports arrived with increasing frequency, to some extent because many Circles were discovered only during harvesting. Even so, during the final week of July and the first week of August, new Circles were appearing at such a rate that I was obliged to hire a plane every few days in a vain attempt to photograph all the new ones in the Wessex area.

Many small formations and even some pictograms were destroyed by harvesting before they were ever recorded. The momentum of the phenomenon at that time was such that it seemed impossible that events would cease solely due to a lack of standing corn. What was happening could really only be appreciated from the air, and the press had by then lost interest as a result of the Bratton hoax. Indeed, Circles were still being reported from the north of England, where the harvest is a few weeks later, long after the corn was out in the south.

First Circles in 1991

Cereologists in Britain awaited the 1991 Circles with anticipation and not a little apprehension. The events of 1990 would be a hard act to follow but we were certain to be in for some surprises. In previous years the Circles had invariably developed new patterns and new facets quite unlike any natural phenomenon, and 1991 was to be no exception.

First report of a Circle came from Butleigh in Somerset where a simple 29-feet swirl appeared in very early wheat that was scarcely a foot high. After the 1990 pictograms such a paltry specimen might scarcely have raised an eyebrow had it not been for the bizarre story which accompanied its formation.

Dave Harris, a local youth, had been riding on a bicycle towards Butleigh when he heard a high-pitched humming sound near an avenue of cedars which crossed the road. Looking up he saw what he described as a silvery bell-shaped craft stationary over the field to his left, perhaps 25 feet from the ground. Below it a spiralling vortex of 'aura-like' light was making a Circle in the crop. Amazed and distracted, he rode the bike into the side of the road, falling off on to the verge. The craft then flew off at high speed and, apart from the hum, all he heard was a swishing noise as it scythed through the air. All this occurred in a very few seconds in broad daylight at 6 p.m. on Sunday, 14 April. He was the only witness.

Naturally such a story was met with ridicule and derision from many, but there is no doubt that this witness had undergone some peculiar experience, whether entirely physical or paranormal. And the Circle itself bore silent testimony to this. Although the farmer and others claimed they 'knew who made it', and even that they 'had seen them do it', the Circle appeared perfectly genuine and dowsed like a genuine Circle. Of course, the very young crop did not exhibit the fine detail which one might expect in a mature one.

Whatever the truth of the matter, this episode provided an interesting exercise in psychology. The plasma vorticists who might have been prepared to accept the Circle as genuine backed off very quickly when they heard this story and what the farmer had to say. Pat Delgado, very wary after the Bratton hoax, quickly labelled this one a hoax. But accomplished dowser Hamish Miller, who arrived long after the event, confidently assured me that this was a genuine Circle. I spoke to Dave Harris at length, and whatever our preconceived ideas about his story, there is no reason to believe that he had fabricated it.

Doubts and Misgivings

These attitudes were to set the tenor of the general perception of many of the formations in 1991. Apart from a few local newspapers, the press took virtually no interest in the pictograms which subsequently appeared, having decided in 1990 that the Crop Circles were no more than elaborate hoaxes and worthy only of silly season attention. Many of the investigators, too, anticipating the possibility of extensive hoaxing, were wary to a fault and rejected many Circles solely on the grounds that they did not look right or did not dowse as they had expected.

In retrospect these attitudes were understandable but they were probably misguided. At the end of 1990 I had been told by George de Trafford that the energies in the 1991 formations would be mostly quite different and that many formations would only prove dowsable on a higher level of dowsing. 'Will you then say', he asked, 'that most of the new formations are fakes?' Confirmation of this prediction was provided on many occasions when no dowsable pattern could be found in some of the 1991 Circles.

Also in 1991 the UFO connection made an unexpected comeback. During several watches mounted in Wiltshire by the various groups studying the phenomenon, there were reports of lights in the sky which did not appear to belong to aircraft or satellites. Unlike Dave Harris' experience at Butleigh, there was never any direct connection between these lights and what appeared in the fields, but it was impossible to discount the suggestion that this was a facet of the Crop Circle phenomenon.

Barbury Castle

At 9 a.m. on 17 July, Richard Wintle, a photographer, was flying to photograph Circles in Wiltshire. He and his pilot flew south of Swindon close to Barbury Castle, an ancient Iron Age hill fort. What they saw in the field below quite took their breath away. A vast pictogram, not unlike a great maze, lay beneath them. Although it was made up of circles and lines, it was completely different from anything that had appeared previously. The sheer geometric precision was so striking that all thoughts that this could have been caused by any sort of natural phenomenon could be dismissed immediately. And the helicopter pilot knew for a fact that this great pattern had not been there at 9 p.m. the previous night.

The photograph of the pictogram (see Plate 1.8) shows that it is centred on a large equilateral triangle which encloses a large double-ringed circle. Beyond the apexes of this triangle are rings or circles, each of a different design. The approximate separation of these is 330 foot.

There is no way that this great pictogram could have resulted from mindless natural forces. I told Dr Meaden this later that day when I met him in the pictogram, adding the question, 'Surely you don't think this was made by an atmospheric vortex, do you?' Although initially reported as saying the formation was far too large and intricate to have been man-made. Dr Meaden eventually stated that it must be a hoax. If he was to sustain his plasma vortex theory he really had no alternative but to say this. Nevertheless, the formation showed all the characteristics of other Circles and pictograms and was strongly dowsable, giving every indication, therefore, that it was genuine.

This particular pictogram was, of course, a watershed. It presented all of us with just one inescapable question: was it man-made? If not, there was absolutely no doubt that we were dealing with some sort of non-human intelligence, whatever form that might take.

Close Encounters

On the night preceding the Barbury Castle finding, Brian Grist from Bristol together with two friends, Gary Hardwick and his girlfriend Alison, were cropwatching near Beckhampton. For more than a month various groups of watchers had stationed themselves in this area where the pictograms had been appearing in the crop-fields. Shortly before midnight Brian and the others noticed lights silently traversing the sky. For the next hour they watched as white lights and lights which pulsed green, red and white moved to the north and to the south of them.

At one stage two of the three saw a large dark object travel overhead at high speed, again in total silence. One of the luminous objects became stationary and stayed in a fixed position for many minutes. There was no possibility that these objects were aircraft and on several occasions the pulsing lights came close to the spot where they were standing. In fact, the three watchers were quite shaken by this extra-ordinary nocturnal display, which was quite unlike anything they had seen before. Brian told me afterwards, 'This was the nearest thing to those scenes in *Close Encounters of the Third Kind* and I just could not believe what was happening.'

Others witnesses cropwatching that night saw similar lights in the sky but I have not had the opportunity to speak to them at the time of writing. Brian and his companions are reliable witnesses and it is clear that something quite extraordinary was happening on the night. Indeed, some of the UFOs were seen in the direction of Barbury Castle.

Other Pictograms

On the same night two other pictograms appeared in this area. One was a helmet-shaped formation near Wootton Bassett, just a few miles away. The other was a long pictogram consisting of circles and rings in line near Preshute Farm on the Marlborough Downs. Out of the end of this pictogram stretched a hand-like protrusion with three fingers. This was similar to the asymmetrical 'keys' and 'claws' of the 1990 pictograms in Wiltshire. When I flew over this last formation on 17 July I was nearly as surprised by what I saw as I had been when I flew over Barbury Castle less than two miles away. At Preshute the whole field was criss-crossed by narrow wavy lines which centred on the pictogram. This was unmis-takably associated with the formation but no cause was apparent. It looked as if dozens of tiny creatures had emerged from the formation and made their way off into the hedges and bushes nearby! This is, of course, fanciful speculation but never had I seen the like of this. There may be some mundane explanation but at present the cause of the tiny trails is completely unknown.

The Circles Continue

It is certainly becoming evident that the Circles are just the outwardly visible sign of some much greater process that is at work, and which is only dimly perceived by the majority of us. According to the dowsers and the psychics who are involved in Circles research, the energies which they detect have been continuously increasing over the last few years, one effect of which is the increasing complexity of the Circle formations. Circles generally form at the intersection of ley energy lines and these lines themselves are said to be multiplying and strengthening. This proliferation of the dowsable lines is said to provide an increasingly complex blueprint for potential Circle formations or pictograms. But the action of the agency which traces out that pattern in the crop, producing the visible circle, and what precipitates that event, remains little understood.

This interpretation of events might be accepted by the materialist were he or she able to detect those dowsable lines with scientific instruments, but in wishing to do this they mistake the true nature of the lines. Dowsable energies are subtle energies whose essential characteristic is their interaction with living things. As such, they directly affect the consciousness of the individual, rather than just his or her body, and thereby produce dowsing reactions, and often other psychic interactions as well. In so far as we are dealing with energies which affect consciousness, these may also embody symbolic forms that are capable of various interpretations. Given that this is the nature of the phenomenon, it is not unexpected, then, that the formations in the fields may also exhibit a symbolic content.

With a further month to run before the harvest, there is no knowing what will come next. If there are more formations like that at Barbury Castle there will be no room for further doubt as to the intelligent nature of this bizarre phenomenon. At present, even the most sceptical have been forced to acknowledge the reality of the Crop Circles as their occurrence spreads worldwide. The 1990 and 1991 pictograms have totally destroyed the theory that they are caused by natural meteorological forces. The evolution continues and only by looking afresh at this phenomenon, without the clutter of preconceived notions, will we be able to understand what is really happening.

Editor's Note

In *The UFO Report 1991* (page 32), George Wingfield reported that a Circle found in Margate, Kent, following a UFO sighting on 10 August 1989, and shown in a photograph which we reproduced, was believed to be a hoax. We have since learned otherwise.

While visiting TV South in Maidstone, Kent, for an interview in August 1990, I was informed by producer Nick Knowles that he had firm evidence that this Circle had been hoaxed. Mr Knowles informed me that a man (possibly called 'Nick') had telephoned him, claiming that he and a group of friends had created the Circle by walking around a central pole with a gradually lowered, outstretched rope, completing the job afterwards by shuffling around the circular area. The caller then stated that he and his friends would repeat this exercise in front of the TVS cameras. However, when TVS telephoned 'Nick' to make arrangements, the man backed down, fearing trouble with the farmer who owned the field where the circle was to be made.

Investigator Paul Harris (who originally informed me that the circle was not a hoax) then made further enquiries, and learned that no record had been kept by TVS of the caller's full name or telephone number, so his identity cannot be checked. In his report on the hoax story, Paul Harris writes as follows:

'... What is known, though, is that the two witnesses to the phenomenon seen on 10 August 1989 thought to have caused the circle were named Wilfred and Simon; names that did not seem familiar to the staff member at TVS. Furthermore, Wilfred Gomez is even now sticking to his story and denies phoning TVS: in fact, all along he has avoided publicity, his experience originally being notified to the newspapers by a friend. The other witness [Simon Millington] has completely avoided all publicity and will not be interviewed. However, all who interviewed Wilfred Gomez are impressed by his sincerity and are inclined to believe his account.

'If the Gomez story has not after all been exposed as a hoax, who was the mystery caller and what was the point in claiming to have created the crop circle in question? It is possible, I suppose, that the circle was artificially created and not related to the phenomenon seen at the same spot by Wilfred Gomez, but this seems to be stretching credulity rather too far! It is much more likely, in my opinion, that the hoax circle claim was prompted by the considerable publicity during 1990 given to crop formations of all types and to those claiming to have made them. Financial rewards offered by national newspapers could have further created an atmosphere encouraging such claims.

'I fear this "hoax" rumour is the result of the sort of mischief-making that currently dogs Circle research, as it has done ufology and related subjects for many years.'

We extend our sincerest apologies to Wilfred Gomez and Simon Millington, and I am grateful to Paul Harris for bringing this matter to my attention. Mr Harris' initial report on this Crop Circle event is published in the *Journal of Meteorology*, Vol. 15, no. 145, January 1990 (edited by Dr G. Terence Meaden).

2

North American Crop Circles in 1990

NORTH AMERICAN INSTITUTE FOR CROP CIRCLE RESEARCH

This study, written by Chris Rutkowski, was conducted by the North American Institute for Crop Circle Research (NAICCR),[1] in conjunction with Ufology Research of Manitoba (UFOROM).[2] Research associates include Roy Bauer, Grant Cameron, Jeff Harland, Gordon Mathews, Walter Nilsson, Chris Rutkowski, Vladimir Simosko and Guy Westcott.

By 1 January 1991, eighty-six Crop Circles and/or physical traces associated with UFO sightings had been reported to UFOROM or otherwise communicated through the NAICCR during the calendar year 1990. These represented forty-five different cases or locations, since in some cases as many as ten separate circles/traces were associated with one location. The physical traces ranged from holes gouged out of the ground to the classic British-style Crop Circle that has become so familiar to the general public through media programmes.

Sixty-one unusual ground markings (UGMs) were found in the United States, and twenty-three reported in Canada. The disproportionately low number in Canada is probably an artefact of the disjointed information network of North America Crop Circle researchers and problems in collecting the data. It is likely that many other cases exist, but the information has yet to reach researchers, for a number of reasons. Indeed, in the case of physical traces associated with UFO sightings, the cases noted in this study are barely representative of the reports throughout North America.

There was no evident trend in the characteristics of the UGMs. Statistical studies conducted on the data did not suggest any particular unifying explanation. The UGMs were classified in the following categories:

(1) flattened circle;
(2) flattened ring;

(3)   burned circle;
(4)   burned ring;
(5)   burned and flattened;
(6)   concentric rings;
(7)   vegetation missing or damaged;
(8)   depression;
(9)   hole(s);
(10) other markings or residue.

The classification system is not mutually exclusive, and in some cases combinations of two or more categories have been found.

If we consider the number of UGMs per category in the United States and Canada, we can note how the cases are distributed. Twice as many flattened circles were found in the United States as Canada, though Canada had many more concentric rings.

There seemed to be a statistical difference in the direction of swirl within Crop Circles. Both clockwise and counter-clockwise swirls were regularly reported, though there was a slight predominance of observed counter-clockwise effects. The difference was minimalized, however, when only one country's UGMs were considered. A direction of swirl was not reported in all cases.

Difficulties with Data

In all analyses, it should be realized that there were problems in the collection and preparation of data. There is a difference between the number of rings found and the number of sites involved, simply because a single site could have a dozen or more Crop Circles associated with it. This is in agreement with the way in which UGM statistics are compiled in Britain and elsewhere. However, this is not entirely satisfying, since in an extreme case where perhaps thirty Circles are found in one field, and it is the only case recorded for that area in a year, it could be argued that there were either thirty Circles found that year, or that there was only one incident reported. By itself, neither statistic reflects the true picture or nature of the phenomenon.

In Canada, the most common crop affected was wheat, whereas grassy fields were most often affected in the United States, though a variety of different crops were affected in the United States, which did not occur in Canada. Flattened circles occurred most often in grass, and were also the victims of 'burns' – another common UGM that may or may not be related to Crop Circles. Concentric circles seemed to form almost exclusively in wheat.

UGM		Total	USA	Canada
(1)	Flattened circle	27	19	8
(2)	Flattened ring	4	3	1
(3)	Burned circle	15	14	1
(4)	Burned ring	3	3	
(5)	Burned and flattened	11	10	1
(6)	Concentric rings	10	1	9
(7)	Vegetation missing	3	2	1
(8)	Depression	1	–	1
(9)	Hole(s)	2	1	1
(10)	Other	2	2	–

Table 2:1. Number of UGMs by category.

	USA	Canada
Clockwise	4	4
Counter-clockwise	10	6

Table 2:2. Direction of swirl (when specified):
clockwise or counter-clockwise.

	Flattened circle	Flattened ring	Concentric rings
Clockwise	14	2	3
Counter-clockwise	4	2	1

Table 2:3. Direction of swirl (when specified) in selected UGM type: clockwise or counter-clockwise.

	Grass	Wheat	Oats	Sorghum	Alfalfa	Corn	Gravel
USA	46	2	3	3	3	1	1
Canada	4	16	–	–	–	–	1

Table 2:4. UGMs per crop ground type

24

	Grass	Wheat	Oats	Sorghum	Alfalfa	Corn	Gravel
FC	14	7	1	3	–	1	–
FR	2	–	2	–	–	–	–
BC	15	–	–	–	–	–	–
BR	–	–	–	–	3	–	–
BF	9	1	–	–	–	–	–
CR	1	9	–	–	–	–	–
VM	3	–	–	–	–	–	–
D	–	–	–	–	–	–	1
H	2	–	–	–	–	–	–
Other	–	1	–	–	–	–	1

Table 2:5. UGM Categories versus crop ground type.

Flattened circles
(diameters in metres)

DATA: 3.3, 3.3, 3.3, 3.3, 3.3, 3.3, 3.3, 3.3, 3.3, 1.7, 18.0, 21.0, 10.0, 20.55, 10.7, 7.7, 18.9, 3.0, 12.05, 38.1, 9.1, 9.1, 18.3, 18.3, 14.2

Average diameter = 10.7 m

(*Note:* For cases where the UGM is elliptical rather than circular, an average of both axes is used for the diameter of the UGM.)

Similarly, from the data given in the case listing, the following
  measurements are determined:

Flattened Rings: average diameter = 9.8 m; average width = 10 cm.
Burned Circles: average diameter = 7.1 m.
Burned rings: average diameter = 4.5 m; average width = 43 cm.
Concentric rings: average diameter = 11.5 m; average width = 62.9 cm.
Burned and Flattened: average diameter = 2.7 m; average width = 22.2 cm.
Vegetation Missing/Damaged: average diameter = 6.3 m; average width =
  65 cm.
Depression: average diameter = 9.1 m; average width = 15 cm.

Figure 2:1. Sizes of UGMs

Classification Problems

This analysis has given us a limited amount of insight into the nature of North American Crop Circles. We can see that a wide a variety of UGMs is being reported, but only about half are popularized by the media. Readers are free to extract other information from the data presented here.

Because the exact cause of the UGMs is still unknown, it is difficult to determine what kinds of data are important. More to the point, it is difficult to ensure that the same information is collected for each case, especially in North America, which is considerably larger than England and much more difficult to cover in terms of investigation teams. It is suspected that the data presented in this study represent only a portion of the total number of cases for 1990, though efforts to obtain the required information were made when and where possible.

It should be remembered that this is a preliminary study of the first 'wave' of Crop Circles in North America, and that the co-ordination of investigations has only just begun. Perhaps the answer is as simple as 'hoax', but many questions arise despite the explanation. What kind of data are required?

This brings up another important question: Are Crop Circles distinguishable from other physical cases? Only a few UGMs noted for 1990 were associated with UFO sightings, which is consistent with the majority of British cases. This is not to say that UFO reports were not made about the same time or in the surrounding region; there were several UFO reports in both Saskatchewan and Manitoba during the period when Crop Circles were found. But the real problem is in the classification of UGMs. Should burned circles be included in the analyses of flattened Crop Circles? What about cases of missing vegetation or soil? Which categories can be considered? The answer is not clear, especially since there are cases on record involving combinations of several categories.

Differences in UGMs

In North America, only a handful of UGMs were anywhere near as complex as the British 'pictograms'. We can, however, note that the British cases seemed to evolve over a considerable period of time: the British Corn Circles have been said to have formally begun in about 1980. It could be suggested that the American versions are simply in an early stage of development. But there are problems with this chronology. It can be shown that there are records of British UGMs dating back much further than 1980: Ted Phillips's trace catalogue shows dozens of British cases during the first half of this century. It would seem logical, then, that an examination of Crop Circles (or UGMs in general) would have to extend backwards into history much further than 1980. This is more evident when we consider American circles and UGMs as well, since again we have records of these phenomena dating back many decades. An early suggestion that the Crop Circles 'started' in Britain

26

and then crossed the Atlantic does not take into account the historical perspective.

Further to this data, it could be suggested that the British Circles are fundamentally different from their American counterparts. This certainly could be true. At the very least, the great numbers of British Circles (between 500 and 1,000, depending on the source) imply that something beyond the American experience is occurring. Some researchers have said that the American circles are hoaxes, whereas the British circles are 'real'. It is obvious that the situation is more complex than that.

It will be noted that this North American sample includes several other kinds of physical traces in addition to the British-style 'Crop Circle'. There are 'burns' and depressions, holes and other effects, not usually considered in the British perspective. This is because American researchers often use the term 'circle' to describe a variety of traces. In addition, some researchers convinced of the UFO connection regard Crop Circles as a subset of physical traces left by the aliens. For the sake of completeness, therefore, it was considered necessary to list all the reported UGMs, regardless of category, but with breakdowns of the numbers in each classification.

UFOs – A Tenuous Connection?

If we begin to consider the various explanations for the Circles, we can be led to a number of different conclusions. It should be apparent that if we include all the reported UGM cases, there will be a combination of hoaxes, natural effects and 'real' phenomena. (Sceptics will argue that the third category is non-existent!)

We can also ask a much more fundamental question: Are Crop Circles of any relevance to UFO research? Some writers have suggested that Crop Circles are not the same kind of phenomena that are considered 'physical traces from UFO landings'. This is in itself a problematic position. Fortean researchers around the world have collected accounts of trace cases over a considerable period of time. The best known of these cases is Ted Phillips's catalogue which in 1975 included about 800 reports of everything from 'angel hair' falls to burned areas following the observation of a 'flying saucer'. Among his collection were many reports of UGMs which we now know more familiarly as Crop Circles: flattened circular patches in grass, grain or other crops. In a number of cases, such a circle was found immediately following the 'take-off' of a 'landed' UFO. Variations included the discovery of a circle some time after the observation of a UFO, but at the spot where the UFO had been seen on the ground, Phillips's collection of data is said presently to number over 4,000 cases.[3]

In our collection of 1990 North American cases, only four of forty-six cases (8.7 per cent) were associated with UFO sightings. It has been suggested that about the same percentage (or smaller) is true for Britain. Despite this, UFOs have been put forward as one explanation for the Crop Circles. Some believe that aliens are 'communicating' with us Earthlings in a peculiar code: the pictograms. A variety of other associated effects have been claimed: unusual noises heard on tape recordings made at Circle sites; malfunctioning of electronic equipment; dowsers report great success at detecting 'earth energy'; animals are said to become agitated or nervous when brought to a circle site. These and other effects are said to indicate that something 'special' is occurring at circle sites – something paraphysical or extraterrestrial.

These effects generally have not been noted at Canadian sites in 1990, and none have been officially reported for the American sites. This does not necessarily mean that such effects do not exist – nor does it necessarily negate the interpretation of the effects as being due to an otherworldly cause. What this *does* mean is that Crop Circles are probably a complex phenomenon with explanations similar to those for their UFO cousins.

Hypotheses

There are four basic explanations for Crop Circles:

(1) extraterrestrials;
(2) wind phenomena;
(3) hoaxes;
(4) other.

The first has already been noted, and is favoured by researchers such as Colin Andrews, Pat Delgado, Michael Chorost and Grant Cameron. The second explanation includes the 'vortex' theories advocated by Terence Meaden, Jenny Randles, Paul Fuller and Guy Westcott. The hoax theory is held by the sceptical members of the Committee for the Scientific Investigation of Claims of the Paranormal (CSICOP). The category of 'other' includes such things as the flattening of crops by mating hedgehogs, the actions of mutant grasshoppers and the result of secret military projects.

It would seem most logical to offer a poststructuralist alternative: it is simple to use deconstructive reasoning to examine all of the above theories. The solution is that no theory is inherently 'wrong', and all

28

theories are 'right'. While this seems a bit unwieldy, consider the arguments as a whole: no one theory adequately explains all of the effects.

We are left with a peculiar collection of data. There can be no denying that Crop Circles were found, but we are faced with unusual ground markings. The easy explanation is that they are hoaxes, but this ignores 'eyewitness' observations of UFOs and also ignores the 'eyewitness' observations of whirlwinds laying cornstalks in neat, circular patterns. We can further ask why no one has claimed the $25,000 (Canadian) or £5,000 rewards if hoaxes are the real answer. And how were the Circles made, really? Is this another planned endeavour by CSICOP to make Ufologists look bad? Are stilts and rollers the instruments of choice?

Or, if winds and vortices are the explanation, then why do Circles form in valleys, hillsides *and* on knolls? Is Britain's change in weather so incredibly dramatic that hundreds of Circles can form in 1990, compared with only a handful a decade ago? And exactly what mechanism is responsible, since the theoretical models proposed to date have been constantly changed to account for the differing conditions and observations of the Circles in such abundance? Why not Alberta, or Delaware?

The 'explanation' that aliens are the culprits is no more satisfying. Why are not more UFOs seen at the Circle sites? Indeed, the absence of accompanying UFO sightings with each Crop Circle site is perhaps the best evidence in support of the contention that Crop Circles are not simply subclasses of physical true cases. Where is the radiation or the non-terrestrial metal? If the aliens are communicating with us, wouldn't there be a better way than pictograms? And yet: Crop Circles do resemble the classic 'saucer nests' like those at Tully and Langenburg many years ago; hoaxes *have* been proven in several cases; winds *are* the cause of many kinds of crop damage.

It seems necessary to consider several alternatives when examining Crop Circles cases (or the broader class of UGMs). It is very likely that any data in support of a natural explanation have been contaminated by hoaxes and other influences. This is quite analogous to the UFO problem itself. Certainly *some* cases are attributable to hoaxes, insects, bolides, aircraft, hallucinations, balloons, kites, birds and other conventional objects. Somewhere, in all of the data, there may be some bona fide UFOs. But which ones?

Below we give the raw, coded data gathered in preparation of this report. The key to the data is given, followed by the data itself, than an annotated list of cases similar in nature to the Phillips catalogue.

Coding Key for Crop Circle Data

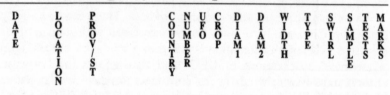

D A T E	L O C A T I O N	P R O V / S T	C O U N T R Y	N U M B E R	U F O	C R O P	D I A M 1	D I A M 2	W I D T H	T Y P E	S W I R L	S A M P L E	T E S T S	M A R K S
900809	SOMEWHERE, SK		CN	01	U	W	15.2	12.8	847	FR	CW	S	T	M

DATE: year/month/day

LOCATION: nearest city, town, village

PROV/ST: province or state

COUNTRY: country

NUMBER: circle/ring number (at site) (i.e. if 3 rings: 01, 02, 03)

UFO: UFO seen at site previous to discovery of physical trace

CROP: affected crop or ground material: A = sorghum, B = beans, C = corn, D = rice, F = alfalfa, G = grass, I = ice, M = marsh, N = cotton, O = oats, P = potatoes, R = gravel, S = snow, T = trees, V = clover, W = wheat, X = sugar beets, Y = tobacco, Z = barley

DIAM1:   major axis of circle/ring (in metres)

DIAM2:   minor axis of circle/ring (in metres)

WIDTH: width of ring (in centimetres)

TYPE: type of physical trace: BC = burned circle, BF = burned and flattened, BR = burned ring, CR = concentric rings, DP = depression, EG = enhanced growth, FC = flattened circle, FR = flattened ring, HO = hole, OT = other, SG = stunted growth, VC = vegetation calcined, VD = vegetation dead, VM = vegetation missing, YG = yellowing of grass

SWIRL: ClockWise or Counter-Clockwise

SAMPLE: samples taken by investigators

TESTS: tests done; results possibly available

MARKS   other markings/traces observed or noted

30

	DATE	LOCATION	PROV/ST	COUNTRY	NUMBER	UFO	CROP	DIAM 1	DIAM 2	WIDTH	TYPE	SWIRL	SAMPLE	TESTS	MARKS
1	900308	MARS, PA		US	01	U	G	02.4	02.5	018	BF		S	T	
2	900308	MARS, PA		US	02	U	G	02.4	02.5	018	BF		S	T	
3	900308	MARS, PA		US	03	U	G	02.4	02.5	018	BF		S	T	
4	900308	MARS, PA		US	04	U	G	02.4	02.5	018	BF		S	T	
5	900308	MARS, PA		US	05	U	G	02.4	02.5	018	BF		S	T	
6	900308	MARS, PA		US	06	U	G	02.4	02.5	018	BF		S	T	
7	900308	MARS, PA		US	07	U	G	02.4	02.5	018	BF		S	T	
8	900308	MARS, PA		US	08	U	G	02.4	02.5	018	BF		S	T	
9	900308	MARS, PA		US	09	U	G	02.4	02.5	018	BF		S	T	
10	900517	FINLEYVILLE, PA		US	01		G	16.5	16.5	060	CR		S	T	
11	900627	WARSAW, IN		US	01		G	03.3	03.3		FC	CC	S	T	
12	900627	WARSAW, IN		US	02		G	03.3	03.3		FC	CC	S	T	
13	900627	WARSAW, IN		US	03		G	03.3	03.3		FC	CC	S	T	
14	900627	WARSAW, IN		US	04		G	03.3	03.3		FC	CC	S	T	
15	900627	WARSAW, IN		US	05		G	03.3	03.3		FC	CC	S	T	
16	900627	WARSAW, IN		US	06		G	03.3	03.3		FC	CC	S	T	
17	900627	WARSAW, IN		US	07		G	01.7	01.7		FC	CC	S	T	
18	900627	WARSAW, IN		US	08		G	03.3	03.3		FC	CC	S	T	
19	901927	WARSAW, IN		US	09		G	03.3	03.3		FC	CC	S	T	
20	900627	WARSAW, IN		US	10		G	03.3	03.3		FC	CC	S	T	
21	900699	BELGRADE, MO		US	01		G				HO				M
22	900699	MILAN, IL		US	01										
23	900708	BIRD'S HILL, MB		CN	01		G				HO				M
24	900799	WILLISTON, ND		US	01	U	G	06.0	06.0		BC				
25	900799	WILLISTON, ND		US	02	U	G	06.0	06.0		BC				
26	900799	WILLISTON, ND		US	03	U	G	06.0	06.0		BC				
27	900799	WILLISTON, ND		US	04	U	G	06.0	06.0		BC				
28	900799	WILLISTON, ND		US	05	U	G	24.0	24.0		BC				
29	900799	WILLISTON, ND		US	06	U	G	24.0	24.0		BC				
30	900806	HURON, SD		US	01		G	03.6	03.6		BC				
31	900806	HURON, SD		US	02		G	03.6	03.6		BC				
32	900806	HURON, SD		US	03		G	06.7	06.7		BC				
33	900806	HURON, SD		US	04		G				BC				
34	900807	LEOLA, SD		US	01		W	18.3	12.2	150	OT				M
35	900810	ALVORD, DESERT, OR		US	01		R	99.9	99.9		OT				M
36	900818	TWEEDSMUIR, SK		CN	01		W	07.6	07.6	060	CR	CW	S	T	
37	900818	ST. FRANCOIS XAVIER, MB		CN	01		W	18.0	18.0		FC	CC	S	T	
38	900822	ROSSER, MB		CN	01		W	21.0	21.0		FC	CC	S	T	
39	900825	CHICORA, PA		US	01		O	09.8	09.7	005	FR	CW			
40	900825	CHICORA, PA		US	02		O	10.4	10.0	005	FR	CW			
41	900825	CHICORA, PA		US	03		O	10.0	10.0		FC	CW			
42	900826	PETERSFIELD, MB		CN	01		W	20.7	20.4		FC	CC			
43	900827	DOMAIN, MB		CN	01		W	10.7	10.7		FC	CW	S	T	

31

	DATE	LOCATION	PROV/ST	COUNTRY	NUMBER	UFO	CROP	DIAM1	DIAM2	WIDTH	TYPE	SWIRL	SAMPLE	TESTS	MARKS
44	900828	NORTHSIDE,	SK	CN	02		W	11.0	11.0	060	CR	CW	S	T	M
45	900828	NORTHSIDE,	SK	CN	01		W	12.2	12.1	060	CR	CW	S	T	M
46	900828	PETERSFIELD,	MB	CN	01		W	07.8	07.6		FC	CC	S	T	
47	900829	NIVERVILLE,	MB	CN	01		W	18.9	18.9		FC	CC	S	T	
48	900831	ALVENA,	SK	CN	01		W	03.3	03.3	122	CR				
49	900831	ALVENA,	SK	CN	02		W	03.3	03.3	122	CR				
50	900831	ALVENA,	SK	CN	03		W	03.3	03.3	122	CR				
51	900831	ALVENA,	SK	CN	04		W	03.3	03.3	122	CR				
52	900899	MEATH PARK,	SK	CN	01		W	09.5	09.2	048	CR	CC			
53	900899	TURTLE LAKE,	ND	US	01	U	G				BC				
54	900899	TURTLE LAKE,	ND	US	02	U	G				BC				
55	900899	TURTLE LAKE,	ND	US	03	U	G				BC				
56	900899	TURTLE LAKE,	ND	US	04	U	G				BC				
57	900899	BRUNKHILD,	MB	CN	01						FC				
58	900899	N.D.-DES-LOURDES,	MB	CN	01										
59	900899	NAPLES,	FL	US	01		G	03.0	03.0		FC				
60	900901	WILLIAMS LAKE,	BC	CN	01	U	R	09.1	09.1	015	DP		S	T	M
61	900901	ST. NORBERT,	MB	CN	01		W	12.2	11.9		FC				
62	900906	LOCKPORT,	MB	CN	01		W	04.6	04.6	060	BF		S	T	M
63	900914	OSCEOLA,	MO	US	01		A	09.1	09.1		FC				
64	900914	ODESSA,	MO	US	01		A	38.1	38.1		FC		S	T	M
65	900914	ODESSA,	MO	US	02		A	09.1	09.1		FC		S	T	M
66	900915	OSKALOOSA,	KS	US	01		G	18.3	18.3		FC				
67	900915	OSKALOOSA,	KS	US	02		G	18.3	18.3		FC				
68	900915	OSKALOOSA,	KS	US	03		G				FC				
69	900923	TWEEDSMUIR,	SK	CN	01										
70	900999	TOPEKA,	KS	US	01										
71	900999	ST-EUGENE,	PQ	CN	01		G	09.1	09.1		BC				
72	900999	STE. AGATHE,	MB	CN	01		W	45.7	45.7	030	CR				
73	900999	CUCAMONGA,	CA	US	01		G				FR				
74	900999	MACON,	IL	US	01										
75	901011	RANDOLPH COUNTY,	NC	US	01		G	09.1	09.1	030	VM		S	T	
76	901016	DAWSON CREEK,	BC	CN	01		G	09.4	09.4	015	FR				
77	901016	MILAN,	IL	US	01		C	14.2	14.2		FC	CW			
78	901021	BARADA,	NE	US	01		F	05.5	05.5	043	BR		S	T	
79	901021	BARADA,	NE	US	02		F	05.5	05.5	043	BR		S	T	
80	901021	BARADA,	NE	US	03		F	03.6	03.6	043	BR		S	T	
81	901099	ASHBORO,	NC	US	01		G								
82	901099	ASHBORO,	NC	US	02		G								
83	901099	ASHBORO,	NC	US	03		G								
84	901099	CHARLOTTE,	NC	US	01		G	05.4	05.4						
85	901099	VALE,	NC	US	01		G				VM				
86	901099	NINGA,	MB	CN	01		G	03.5	03.5	100	VM				

32

Annotated Listing of 1990 UGM Cases

1. 900308   Mars, PA   Nine unusual markings were found in a grassy field. The oval 'burns' were approximately 2.4 m in diameter, and were aligned in a row. Around the edges of each 'circle' was a ring of depressed grass about 18 cm in width. A pink, glowing light was seen hovering in the area prior to the rings' discovery. Source: Stan Gordon, PASU.

2. 900517   Finleyville, PA   Two concentric rings surrounding a bare circle were found in a grassy field. The rings were not evident two days prior to discovery. There were no tracks leading into or out of the area. The outer ring was 16.5 m in diameter, the middle ring was 12.1 m, and the inner circle was 1.8 m. The outer ring was 60 cm in width and the middle ring was 123 cm. Source: Stan Gordon PASU.

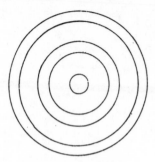

Case 2: Finleyville, pa.

3. 900627   Warsaw, IN   Ten circles were found on a subdivision lot by a man who was picking raspberries. The circles were ignored until early October when reports of other circles in the region were publicized. The circles ranged in diameter from 1.7 to 3.3 m, and were in a field of metre-high grass and shrubs. All had an even, counter-clockwise spiral pattern. Source: Lucius Farish.

4. 900699   Belgrade, MO   A hole was found in a field. There was a 'small crater with three holes in it'. No other details available. Source: Grant Cameron.

5. 900699   Milan, IL   A Crop Circle was found. No other information. Source: Grant Cameron.

6. 900708   Bird's Hill, MB   An unusual hole and effects were found in a field as farmers were baling hay. RCMP and UFOROM investigated. The hole was thought to have been caused by a lightning strike. Source: UFOROM.

7. 900799   Williston, ND   Six 'burned circles' were found in the extreme western part of North Dakota. Ranchers brought the markings to the attention of researchers in August 1990. The circles ranged in size from 6 m to 24 m in diameter. UFOs had been seen in the area during the time the circles were thought to have been created. Source: John Salter.

8.   900806   Huron, SD   Four strange circles of darkened or 'burned' grass were found over a period of two weeks. They ranged from 3.6 m to 6.7 m in diameter. Source: Grant Cameron and MUFON.

9.   900807   Leola, SD   A marking in the shape of a 'backwards question mark' was found in a wheat field by a grain elevator worker who observed it from the top of the bin. There were three rectangular marks spaced around the main pattern. The entire affected area was 18.3 m by 12.2 m in size. Source: MUFON and UFOROM.

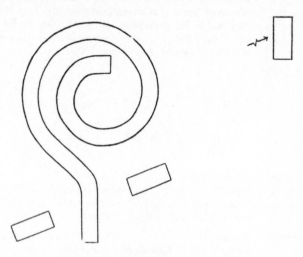

Case 9: Leola, S. Dak.

10.   900810   Alvord Desert, OR   An immense 'pictograph' of a 'sriyantra' (mantra) was found ploughed into a dry lake bed. It was discovered by pilots of the Idaho National Guard. The marking was over 400 m in diameter and contained over nearly 25 km of precisely formed curves. An artist has claimed responsibility. Source: various.

11.   900818   Tweedsmuir, SK   A flattened circle with a concentric ring was found in a wheat field, swirled clockwise. The central circle was 3.6 m in diameter, surrounded by a ring of standing grain, then a ring of crushed grain 7.6 m in diameter and 60 cm in width. Source: Grant Cameron and Chad Deetkin.

12.   900818   St Francois Xavier, MB   A circle of flattened grain was found, swirled counter-clockwise. Its diameter was 18 m, and it was only about the same distance away from a Provincial Highway. The circle was found when a farmer began a swathing pass. There were no signs of entry into the field. Source: UFOROM.

13.   900822   Rosser, MB   A circle of flattened grain was found, swirled counter-clockwise. Its diameter was 21 m, and it was about 30 m away from the nearest access road. There were no signs of entry into the field. Source: UFOROM.

34

14. 900825   Chicora, PA   A flattened circle was found in an oat field. Ill-defined but overlapping rings were found as well. All appeared swirled in a clockwise direction. The main circle was 10 m in diameter; the rings were slightly elliptical: one had axes of 10.4 m and 10 m, and the other had axes of 9.8 m and 9.7 m. Their widths were 5 cm. Source: Stan Gordon, PASU.

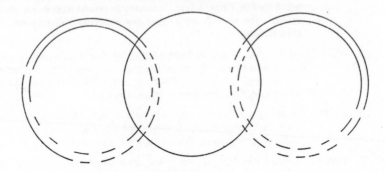

Case 14: Chicora, Pa.

15. 900826   Petersfield, MB   A farmer and his son found a flattened circle while preparing to swath. The circle was slightly elliptical, with axes 7.8 m and 7.6 m. It was located well away from the nearest access road; no signs of entry into the field were found. Source: UFOROM.

16. 900827   Domain, MB   A circular swirled pattern was found in a wheat field. Its diameter was 10.7 m, and it was located near an access road. The grain appeared 'woven' in a clockwise direction. Source: UFOROM.

17. 900828   Northside, SK   A flattened circle with two concentric rings was found, with a trail leading to two additional small flattened areas. Four 'spokes' radiated from the centre of the main circle. A second circle was nearby, about 125 m away behind a bluff of trees. The larger formation was elliptical, with axes 12.2 m and 12.1 m, while the other was circular and 11 m in diameter. Source: UFOROM, media and Chad Deetkin.

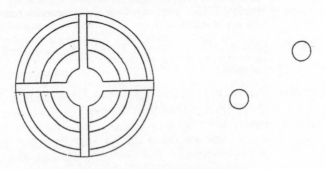

Case 17: Northside, Sask.

35

18. 900828   Petersfield, MB   A slightly elliptical swirled impression was found in a wheat field, swirled counterclockwise. Its axes were 7.8 m and 7.6 m. The farmers who discovered the 'circle' were adamant that there were no tracks leading into the area. Source: UFOROM.

19. 900829   Niverville, MB   Although not there the previous evening, a Crop Circle was found in a wheat field. Its diameter was 18.9 m, and it was swirled counter-clockwise. A slight depression was visible in the centre. Source: UFOROM.

20. 900831   Alvena, SK   A ring of flattened grain was found, surrounding a small tuft of standing wheat. The entire diameter was only 3.3 m, and the width of the ring was 122 cm. In the surrounding fields, three more similar rings were found. Source: media and Chad Deetkin.

21. 900899   Meath Park, SK   A concentric ring and circle formation was found. The inner circle was 5.9 m in diameter; the ring had axes of 9.5 m and 9.2 m and was 48 cm in width. Source: media and Chad Deetkin.

22. 900899   Turtle Lake, ND   Ranchers had seen bright lights in a field, then discovered some 'burned circles' a few days later. Source: John Salter.

23. 900899   Brunkhild, MB   A circle of flattened wheat was said to have been discovered near this town. Source: Don Johnson.

24. 900899   Notre-Dame-des-Lourdes. MB   It was claimed that a Crop Circle was discovered near this town. Source: CBWFT-TV.

25. 900899   Naples, FL   A man reported finding a flattened circle in tall grass 'in the Everglades, not too far out of town'. The circle was about 3 m in diameter, and formed in metre-high weeds in a dried-up lake bed. Source: Grant Cameron.

26. 900901   Williams Lake, BC   A strange depressed ring appeared on a gravel driveway. It was 9.1 m in diameter, and 15 cm wide. The gravel in the affected area was pressed about 5 cm into the ground, and seemed 'pulverized' at some points. That same night, a strange glowing light was seen nearby. Other effects reported. Source: Michael Strainic.

27. 900901   St Norbert, MB   A circular marking was found in a field of swathed wheat. It was 4.6 m in diameter, and the wheat seemed to have been 'shredded'. After some investigation, a farmhand admitted his hoax. Source: UFOROM.

28. 900906   Lockport, MB   A patch of stunted growth, 3.3 m in diameter, was found surrounded by a ring of flattened grain about 60 cm wide. Source: UFOROM.

29. 900914   Osceola, MO   A Crop Circle about 9 m in diameter was found in a sorghum field. Source: MUFON.

30. 900914   Odessa, MO   Two large, generally circular formations were found in a sorghum field near Kansas City. The larger was 38 m in diameter, and the smaller was about 9 m in diameter. The formations 'grew' projections into the surrounding crop over a period of a few days. Source: MUFON.

31. 900915   Oskaloosa, KS   Three circles were found in a grassy field. Two were 18.3 m in diameter, while the third was somewhat smaller. Source: MUFON.

32. 900923   Tweedsmuir, SK   Another Crop Circle was found near this town. Source: media.

33. 900999   Topeka, KS   One Crop Circle was found. Source: MUFON.

34. 900999   St-Eugene, PQ   A cottager found a 'burnt circle' near his cabin. It was about 9 m in diameter, and was in grass. It was claimed that a similar ring had been found there last year. Source: CBWFT-TV.

35. 900999   Ste Agathe, MB   A pair of concentric rings was found. They were narrow, circular tracks, about 30 cm in width, somehow cut into the field. The smaller was 27 m in diameter, and the outer ring was 46 m. Source: CBWFT-TV.

36. 900999   Cucamonga, CA   A woman reported that there was a half-circle in her front lawn, 'pressed down'. Source: Grant Cameron.

37. 900999   Macon, IL   It was reported that Crop Circles were found in fields near this town. Source: Grant Cameron.

38. 901011   Randolph County, NC   A large ring was found in a grassy field during the same time that a loud noise and bright lights were reported by residents of the region. The ring was about 9 m in diameter and about 30 cm wide. Source: Lucius Farish.

39. 901016   Dawson Creek. BC   A ring of flattened grass was found in a field. Its diameter was 9.4 m and its width was 15 cm. Source: Michael Strainic.

40. 901016   Milan, IL   A circular area of flattened corn was found, with a diameter of 14.2 m The ground was flat, 'as if the furrows had been pressed out'. The corn was laid in a clockwise direction. Source: UFOROM and Edith Ashley.

41. 901021   Barada, NB   Two rings were found on the side of a hill; a third was found a few days later. The first two were 5.5 m in diameter, and the other was 3.6 m. All were about 45 cm in width. The rings were 'burnt brown' in an otherwise healthy crop. 'Violet root rot' was suggested as the cause. Source: Lucius Farish.

42. 901099   Ashboro, NC   Three UGMs were found. No other information available. Source: MUFON.

43. 901099   Charlotte, NC   A circle with a diameter of about 5.5 m was discovered. Source: MUFON.

44. 901099   Vale, NC   A 'fungus ring' was found. Source: MUFON.

45. 901099   Ninga, MB   A 'completely bald patch' was found at the top of a grassy knoll. It was in the shape of a ring, and was 3.5 m in diameter with normal grass in the centre. Source: Jeff Harland and Miles Phillips.

REFERENCES
1. North American Institute for Crop Circle Research, 649 Silverstone Avenue, Winnipeg, Manitoba, Canada R3T 2V8.
2. Ufology Research of Manitoba, P.O. Box 1918, Winnipeg, Manitoba, Canada, R3C 3R2.
3. Phillips, Ted: *Physical Traces Associated with UFO Sightings*, Center for UFO Studies, Chicago 1975.

3

British Official UFO Reports from the 1950s

NICHOLAS REDFERN

Born in 1964, Nicholas Redfern has been interested in the subject of UFOs for a number of years and has concentrated his investigations on obtaining official documentation from England and abroad. Having obtained many thousands of pages of official reports released by various governments, he is convinced that there is an active alien presence on Earth, and that there is a concerted effort on the part of a number of countries to keep this information classified.

Nicholas Redfern is currently employed as assistant manager for a home improvement company. Should any readers have information which has a bearing on this article, Mr Redfern can be contacted at: 20 Paradise Lane, Pelsall, Walsall, West Midlands WS3 4NH, England.

That the Government of the United States of America has been, and continues to be, intimately involved in the subject of Unidentified Flying Objects is now proven beyond doubt. Documentation released under the terms of the US Freedom of Information Act shows that numerous government agencies are implicated in this bizarre subject, including the Central Intelligence Agency, the National Security Agency, the Federal Bureau of Investigation, the Defense Intelligence Agency and the Atomic Energy Commission, to name but a handful.

The National Security Agency, which was the subject of several lawsuits in respect of its UFO files, admitted as recently as 1989 that it has continued to monitor UFO reports throughout the whole of the 1980s, and that to release the information acquired would cause 'exceptionally grave damage to the national security. Because the documents are currently and properly classified, they are exempt from disclosure.'[1]

Less easy to prove is high-level involvement on the part of the British Government. The Ministry of Defence's current public attitude is that they will only investigate UFO sightings to determine whether or not the occurrences are a threat to the security and defence of the United Kingdom. The MoD state that 'this is not normally the case and no attempt is made by the MoD to investigate or identify the objects'.[2]

Despite this public stance, my article will attempt to show, via important new documentation and first-hand witnesses, that there has been, and continues to be, intense involvement on the part of the British Government. The fact that the United Kingdom has no Freedom of Information Act means that the general public can only gain access to documents when they are released under the thirty-year ruling. Even then, the Government often withholds papers if it deems this necessary [sometimes for 100 years, or even indefinitely – Ed.]. Despite this, certain information which has recently come to light suggests that the British Government has conducted extensive investigations of UFO sightings since at least September 1952, and that it has endeavoured to keep this data classified in spite of various protestations.

The Topcliffe Case

On 9 August 1952, the Air Ministry stated that a 'full intelligence study' had determined that all reported UFO incidents could be attributed to hoaxes, optical illusions, mistaken identities and known astronomical phenomena. This intelligence study was apparently carried out in 1951 and the above statements were made following an enquiry on the part of the then Prime Minister, Winston Churchill.[3]

Despite this, an event occurred barely a month after the Air Ministry's statement which was to alter radically the British Government's attitude towards the subject of UFOs. This case, generally known as the 'Topcliffe Incident', took place on 19 September 1952. A document signed by Flight Lieutenant Dolphin of RAF Topcliffe, Yorkshire, to Headquarters, No. 18 Group, and dated 20 September 1952, states: 'In accordance with your instructions, herewith a report on the unidentified object which was seen over the station earlier today.' The report referred to was prepared by one of the primary witnesses to the event – Flight Lieutenant John Kilburn – and reads as follows:

Sir,
  I have the honour to report the following incident which I witnessed on Friday, 19th September. I was standing [illegible] with four other aircrew personnel of No. 269 Squadron watching a Meteor fighter gradually descending. The Meteor was at approximately 5,000 feet and approaching from the east. Paris suddenly noticed a white object in the sky at a height between ten and twenty thousand feet some five miles astern of the Meteor. The object was silver in colour and circular

40

in shape; it appeared to be travelling at a much slower speed than the Meteor but was on a similar course.

It maintained the slow forward speed for a few seconds before commencing to descend, swinging in a pendulum motion during descent, similar to a falling sycamore leaf. This was at first thought to be a parachute or engine cowling. The Meteor, meanwhile, turned towards Dishforth and the object, while continuing its descent, appeared to follow suit. After a few seconds, the object stopped its pendulous motion and its descent, and began to rotate about its own axis. Suddenly it accelerated at an incredible speed towards the west, turning onto a south easterly heading before disappearing. All this occurred in a matter of fifteen to twenty seconds. The acceleration was in excess of that of a shooting star. I have never seen such a phenomenon before. The movements of the object were not identifiable with anything I have seen in the air and the rate of acceleration was unbelievable.

Flight Officer R. N. Paris, Flight Lieutenant M. Cybulski, Master Sergeant Thompson, Sergeant Dewis and Leading Aircraftsman Grimes, all of No. 269 Squadron, were with me at the time and witnessed the phenomenon concur with this report. The weather conditions at the time were clear skies, sunshine and unlimited visibility.

I have the honour to be, Sir, Your obedient Servant J. Kilburn, Flight Lieutenant, No. 269 Squadron.

As well as the military sightings mentioned above, a number of reports made by civilians were forwarded to RAF Topcliffe. A document formerly classified 'Confidential', dated 25 September 1952, states that

A report has already been sent to you under reference of letter TOP/C 16/AIR, dated 20 September 1952, concerning the sighting of a 'Flying saucer' by personnel at this station. Since this report was despatched, letters have been received from persons resident in the York area at 20 and 35 miles from here, stating they saw a similar object. A further letter has been received from a man living at Waterhouses, County Durham, saying that he witnessed a similar incident in May, 1950. Letters of thanks for their information have been sent to these three men.

This was signed by J. A. C. Stratton, Group Captain, Officer Commanding, RAF Topcliffe.

The Government was sufficiently concerned by this incident to forward an official report on the event to the Commander-in-Chief, Air/East Atlantic, a NATO subdivision, which states as follows:

Following unusual incident observed RAF Topcliffe by number officers and airmen aircrew 191053 local time. Meteor aircraft observed at approx. 500 feet and descending. White object was seen 5 miles astern at approx. 15000 feet and moving at comparatively slow speed on similar course. Object was silver in colour and circular. It maintained slow forward speed before commencing descent. Swinging in pendulum motion like a sycamore leaf. Thought by observers to be parachute or cowling from Meteor aircraft. Aircraft had turned towards Dishforth and object. Whilst still descending, appeared to follow suit. Pendulous motion and descent ceased and object began rotary motion about its own axis. Suddenly accelerated at an incredible speed in a westerly direction but turning to a S.E. course. Observers stated that the movements were not identifiable with anything they had seen in the air and acceleration was in excess of that of a shooting star. Duration of incident 15/20 seconds.

Copies of this official report were forwarded to a number of government departments, namely the Chief of the Air Staff, the Assistant Chief of the Air Staff, the Secretary of State and the Ministry of Defence's Directorate of Scientific Intelligence.[4]

Operation Mainbrace

At the same time as the events at Topcliffe were occurring, a highly significant NATO exercise called 'Mainbrace' was taking place during the period 13–24 September 1952 in the north-east Atlantic and the North Sea, involving the forces of a number of countries. The US presence in this exercise was largely represented by the aircraft carrier *USS Franklin D. Roosevelt*, which was under the overall command of Vice Admiral Felix B. Stump.

Detailed records of the involvement of the *Roosevelt* in Mainbrace have been made available under the Freedom of Information Act. According to the records, the exercise began 'the extensive development of NATO procedures, which still is a major concern of COM-STRIKFLTLANT in training and integration of the various national forces into a NATO fleet'. Clearly the exercise was highly significant.

What is known is that on 20 September (one day after the Topcliffe incident) an American press photographer, Wallace Litwin, who was on board the *Roosevelt*, obtained a number of photographs of a silver, circular object which was manoeuvring above the fleet. Extensive checks were made to determine if this could be a military vehicle of some kind. The answer was negative.

A further sighting occurred on 21 September. Again, the object was reported to be silver and circular. This time, however, an interception was attempted by a number of RAF fighter planes engaged in the exercise. The UFO was able easily to outdistance itself from the planes.[5]

Extensive files on Mainbrace exist within the papers held at the Public Record Office at Kew, London. A number give useful background information as well as detailing the Russian response to the exercise. One file in particular, entitled 'Operation Mainbrace: Reports on possible repercussions in Denmark', is closed for fifty years. Whether further relevant information may be contained in this file is open to speculation.[6]

RAF Neatishead, Norfolk

Further corroboration for this series of events has come from an individual who at the time of the Topcliffe and Mainbrace incidents was stationed at RAF Neatishead, Norfolk.

Senior Aircraftsman F. W. R. (name and documents verifying his position at Neatishead are on file), who was employed as a radar mechanic, states as follows:

> The main radar equipment at Neatishead was CHL Type 7 Metric, a large rotating aerial. A mobile equivalent, AMES Type, was basically the same but was capable of being towed by lorries.
>
> I was on duty early one morning during the Mainbrace exercise. Sometime between the hours 0400 to 0800 an object was picked up on our scopes flying over the North Sea and parallel to the English coast. The height/range display gave its height as being in excess of 50,000 feet. Meteors and Venoms were scrambled from Coltishall [a nearby base] as the object was not identifiable. When the planes headed across the sea to attempt to intercept it, the object rapidly accelerated and disappeared from our screens heading on a target for Norway. None of the planes got close enough to record a visual contact.
>
> The next day a photographic team arrived, from Coltishall I think, whose job it was to fit the Plan Position Indicator (P.P.I.) tube with a camera. The next day a similar event occurred and an object was picked up on the scope, and again planes were scrambled. The object accelerated out of range and the aircraft were forced to give up the chase. This time, however, the plots of the object and the planes on the radar were all recorded by the camera.
>
> We were never given any explanation as to what had occurred nor were we told where the photographic material was sent. The object never returned.

F. W. R. went on to state that the incidents were 'the talk of the camp'. The fact that the decision was made to set up a camera after the first day's events is intriguing. It suggests that a return 'visit' was anticipated.[7]

The Deputy Directorate of Intelligence

According to newspaper reports of the time, the Air Ministry was still unable to explain the sightings at Topcliffe eleven weeks after the event.[8] The press statements reveal that 'the special branch dealing with this is keeping an open mind on the subject and all reports received are still being studied'. The 'special branch' referred to here is most likely the Deputy Directorate of Intelligence, Technical Branch, from hereon referred to as DDI (Tech.). Important documentation has recently been released which throws further light on DDI involvement in UFO studies.

A little more than a month after the aforementioned report was issued – on 13 January 1953 – Fighter Command Headquarters issued a document outlining procedures to be taken in the event that unusual aerial phenomena should be detected on radar. It is highly probable that this was as a result of the events at Neatishead approximately four months previously.

A further document, dated 16 December 1953, shows the Government's concern with regard to its investigations of UFO sightings. The document, entitled *Reports on Aerial Phenomena*, states the following:

1. It has been decided that sightings of aerial phenomena by Royal Air Force personnel are in future to be reported in writing by Officers Commanding Units immediately and direct to Air Ministry, (DDI (Tech.)), with copies to Group and Command Headquarters. In addition, any reports from civilians received by units should be acknowledged formally in writing and copies of the reports themselves forwarded direct to Air Ministry, (DDI (Tech.)).

2. It will be appreciated that the public attach more credence to reports by Royal Air Force personnel than to those by members of the public. *It is essential that the information should be examined at Air Ministry and that its release should be controlled officially. All reports are, therefore, to be classified 'Restricted' and personnel are to be warned that they are not to communicate to anyone other than official persons any information about phenomena they have observed, unless officially authorised to do so* [emphasis added].

3. This procedure does not apply to the radar detection of unusual targets which is to be reported through the normal channels as required by Fighter Command Headquarters letter FC/S.45485/Signals, dated 13th January, 1953.

This particular document, which was prepared by Flight Lieutenant C. P. B. Russell for Senior Air Staff Officer No. 11 Group, received wide distribution. Clearly this was a change from the Air Ministry's 1952 remarks concerning 'hoaxes, optical illusions', etc.

An update to this document, dated 6 December 1956, includes a number of amendments. Classified 'Secret', the document stated that all reports were henceforth to be classified 'Confidential'. Also included are detailed instructions for reporting radar sightings of UFOs. To quote from the document in question:

Radar detection of unusual targets is to be reported by stations through the normal channels. They should make a special report of any unusual response, i.e. any responses moving at a ground speed exceeding 700 knots, at any height and at any speed above 60,000 feet. When an unusual response is seen, the supervisor or NCO in charge of the watch should be informed and he should then check that the echo is not spurious, and arrange for the necessary records to be made to provide the information listed in paragraph 6 below.

Paragraph 6 states that:

> Reports on such phenomena should contain a personal assessment of, and where applicable, a copy of, the following:
> (A) appearance of the echo.
> (B) the signal strength of the echo (strong, medium and weak) throughout the time of the observation, including pick-up and fade points.
> (C) range and bearing by initial plot and fade points.
> (D) ground speed.
> (E) whether painting of echo is continuous or intermittent.
> (F) a copy of the record sheets, together with a track tracing.

This highly important document, prepared by Squadron Leader G. D. Edwards, again received a wide distribution. The abovementioned papers seem to have been implemented in January 1953. It is most probable that this was as a direct result of the events of September 1952.[9]

The Directorate of Scientific Intelligence

Mention has been made above of the Defence Ministry's Directorate of Scientific Intelligence (DSI). Certainly DSI was provided with a copy of the official report on Topcliffe. But is there any evidence to suggest deeper involvement on the part of DSI? I have made a concerted effort to answer this question and it is worth quoting a number of statements made by the Public Record Office (PRO) in respect of this quest.

'The records of the Defence Ministry's Scientific Intelligence Branch, Public Record Office class reference DEFE 21 are under arrangement and so are not available for general access as yet,' I was informed in 1990. 'It is possible that some documents contained in this class may become available for inspection in 1991. Please also note that because of the nature of these files many will be under extended closure and so closed for 50, 75 or 100 years.'[10]

I pursued this further, specifically with regard to the DSI and its possible involvement with UFO studies. This brought forth the following from the PRO:

> The records currently under arrangement at MoD are of (a) the Scientific and Technical Intelligence Branch (STIB) and (b) the Directorate of Scientific Intelligence (DSI). The activities of the former would not have embraced UFOs and whilst the latter may have, their records are concerned with DSI's relationship with STIB and matters which do not extend to UFOs. Whether material touching on the subject of your enquiry survives amongst the 1950s record of DSI and, if so, whether it would be made available, is not within my knowledge, and I have

therefore passed a copy of this letter and the related correspondence to the MoD
Departmental Record Officer for consideration[11]

In their reply, the Ministry of Defence stated:

> The Public Record Office Inspecting Officer advised you, in his letter . . . that your
> enquiry regarding a particular piece within Class DEFE 21 was being passed to the
> MoD Departmental Record Officer (DRO), for consideration. I can now advise
> you that an examination of the pieces listed under DEFE 21 revealed that the
> earliest anything might be released is in 1993. In the meantime, I am afraid that I
> am unable to comment on the content of the material due to be released. I am sorry
> to have given you such a disappointing reply.[12]

Whether or not any relevant UFO data concerning DSI will one day be
released does of course remain to be seen. In the meantime, the above
remains food for thought. However, there are several points which
should be raised.

The Topcliffe, Neatishead and Mainbrace events certainly seem to
confirm the hypothesis that unknown aerial vehicles were operating in
and around British airspace at a time when highly significant military
exercises were taking place. More importantly, these objects remained
unidentified. Why should DSI be involved? It is known that DSI had
obtained extensive files on Soviet rocket research which the Soviet
Union had obtained from German scientists captured at the end of the
Second World War. Therefore the possibility exists that DSI was
interested in determining whether there were any technical advances
that could be made from studying UFO reports. Given their interest in
rocket technology, this seems reasonable. Unfortunately, since we have
no way at present of gaining access to DSI files, we can only speculate as
to their involvement. Despite this, we may be a step closer to under-
standing the British Government's attitude towards UFO studies in the
early 1950s.

CIA Corroboration of Mainbrace Events?

Further confirmation for the events of September 1952 may exist within
the files of the American Central Intelligence Agency (CIA). Among
the many pages of UFO-related documents released by the CIA in the
late 1970s are a large number of foreign newspaper reports. One case in
particular may have a bearing on the incidents described above.

As part of their routine monitoring of foreign press agencies, the CIA
obtained a copy of a Norwegian newspaper clipping concerning an
incident that occurred on 18 September 1952. The CIA stated that the

report was published in a four-times-a-week newspaper in Harstad, Norway. A translation of the article gives us the following information:

> On 18 September, at 1400 hours, three forestry workers who were working right outside Kirkenes noticed a flat, round object hovering motionless at about 500 meters altitude. The object appeared to have a diameter of 15–20 meters. After the workers had observed the object for a while, it suddenly flew away at great speed in a northwesterly direction. It appears that only these workers saw the object; they swear, however, that their report is true.

On the face of it this would seem to be a fairly typical UFO report. However, there are three points worth considering:

(1) The incident occurred on 18 September, one day before the Topcliffe and Mainbrace events began.
(2) The characteristics of the Norwegian object are similar to those reported during Mainbrace and at Topcliffe.
(3) The fact that this incident occurred over Norway may be of significance, given the statement made by the individual from RAF Neatishead who recalled that the object reported by him was lost as it was on a heading for Norway.

The pronounced lack of British reports found within the CIA's released files suggests the possibility that some sort of prior arrangement on the part of the British Government and the CIA has been made to withhold certain papers. Therefore, further corroborating data may exist within the files of the CIA.

Conclusions

What can be concluded from the events of September 1952?

The fact that following these incidents the Government implemented new guidelines for the reporting of UFO sightings is highly significant. The aforementioned DDI papers show how seriously the Government took the subject of UFOs and how anxious it was that the information should remain classified and that its release should be 'controlled officially'.

Many other reports exist within the files at the PRO which show that the DDI undertook intense study on this subject throughout the late 1950s. Is there any evidence to suggest that a similar situation exists today? As mentioned earlier, the Ministry of Defence states that its involvement in the subject is extremely limited. However, certain information has come to light in the past year that suggests otherwise.

In 1990, the MoD stated that 'such reports are passed to staff in the departments concerned with the UK's air defences, who would examine them as part of their normal duties, in order to determine whether or not any threat to defences had occurred'.[13] An attempt to determine which actual 'departments' are involved brought the following response: 'I regret that on this occasion there is nothing I can usefully add to my letter of 30 April.'[14] Clearly, the MoD is careful not to release too much information which could counter its public stance.

While we do not know the Government's conclusions on the events of September 1952, we may now be getting closer to the truth – a truth which could prove startling for us all.

REFERENCES
1. Confirmation for the ongoing monitoring of UFO reports on the part of the National Security Agency came via correspondence dated 22 May, 31 May and 21 August 1989.
2. Letter from the Ministry of Defence, 23 March 1988.
3. For further details see Good, Timothy: *Above Top Secret: The Worldwide UFO Cover-up*, Sidgwick & Jackson, London 1987; Grafton Books, London 1988.
4. Information on the Topcliffe events comes via documentation released by the Public Record Office, Kew, Richmond, Surrey, TW9 4DU. The second document cited here is reproduced in the appendix of *Above Top Secret*.
5. Information relating to Operation Mainbrace was released by the US Navy under the terms of the Freedom of Information Act.
6. Information supplied by the Public Record Office.
7. Interview, 16 January 1991.
8. *Sunday Dispatch*, 7 December 1952.
9. DDI papers released in the last two years.
10. Letter from the Public Record Office, 21 September 1990.
11. Ibid., 18 December 1990.
12. Letter from the Ministry of Defence, 8 January 1991.
13. Ibid., 30 April 1990.
14. Ibid., 8 January 1991.

Editor's Note

We are indebted to the Public Record Office, Kew, for permission to publish extracts from the following documents held in their custody: AIR 16/1199, AIR 20/7390, AIR 20/9994. *(Crown copyright.)*

4
The Chinese Scene 1990–91

PAUL DONG

Paul Dong was born in Canton, China, in 1928, but now lives in Oakland, California. He has been studying the UFO phenomenon for many years and has written many articles for newspapers and journals in China, and a number of books, including *The Four Major Mysteries of Mainland China* and *UFOs over Modern China*.

In 1981 Paul Dong lectured on UFOs throughout China, speaking to packed audiences at the Peking Ching Hua University Students Union, Canton Science Museum, Canton Jinan University and elsewhere.

Mr Dong is an editor of the Chinese language magazine *Journal of UFO Research*. He can be contacted at PO Box 2011, Oakland, California 94604.

Some say that the appearances of UFOs are regularly scheduled events, but I disagree. There is no order from an extraterrestrial command centre concerning the schedule of visits, and there is no preference for the Americas. If a UFO were to visit Moscow's Red Square for several days in a row, that might be no more than coincidence, especially considering that not all UFOs are extraterrestrial in origin: some may be mere geological emanations from the Earth, appearing and disappearing at random.

China's 'UFO fever' has chilled over the past year or so, but in spite of that, the large increase in UFO news in China was rather abnormal. Below I provide several examples for your study.

Huangshi, Hubei Province

At 10.10 on the evening of 28 March 1990, four UFOs appeared in the region of Huangshi, Hubei Province. As Mei Qi, a reader of the *Journal of UFO Research*, reported at the time:

'Just as I was doing "qi gong" exercises on a vacant lot next to the gymnasium, I suddenly noticed a line of bright lights moving overhead.

49

As I looked up, I was astonished: before my eyes, at a distance of about a thousand metres, four points of light, evenly spaced and forming a line, were moving from east to west at a not very high speed. The two lights at the back were both followed by what looked like comets' tails connected to them, and this gave them a long, winding form. Every so often dazzling lights flashed from within them. The two lights in front, however, were very sharply defined and had no tails.

'After flying about one minute, these four lights disappeared in the expanse of the eastern night sky. There was not a sound during the entire time, other than a few voices from people in the vicinity crying, "Flying saucer! Flying saucer!"

'The next day, when I asked my colleagues whether any of them had seen the spectacle of the previous evening, a Mr Peng said that he had too, and he even submitted a report to the radio station. As we were discussing what sort of objects the four lights were, Mr Peng said they could not have been airplanes, because they didn't have navigation lights, and besides, they were flying so low and not making a sound. They could not have been shooting stars, either, because they didn't fall.

'Some said they could have been signal lights released by peasants. If that were the case, there would be no explanation for the way the four lights were spaced so evenly and moving so smoothly, and the tails on the third and fourth lights (the trail of light to the west) appeared to be flying against the wind. How could signal lights fly against the wind with no power of their own? Several comrades who had seen the lights were puzzled: they had never seen anything like it before. Could this have been a case of those legendary unidentified flying objects?'

Sihong County, Jiangsu Province

On 7 July 1990, Hi Jiyun, a teacher in Taiping High School, Sihong County, Jiangsu Province, returned home for summer vacation and was hoeing a field with his family when a strange phenomenon occurred. He reported:

'At the time the whole field was filled with a large number of people hoeing. Suddenly, someone shouted, "The sun has two sparks!" As I looked up, indeed it was so. This was at 6.50 p.m. I also noticed that to the upper right of the sun was a little black cloud with many stars around its edge. While the cloud sailed off to the east, some of us counted that there was a total of sixteen "stars".

'At the time, the sky was spotlessly clear except for a few tiny clouds on the eastern horizon. Even though the sun was blinding, the silver-

white flashes of the "stars" were dazzling, and they were also constantly shifting, but these transformations were restricted to a fairly
small sector of the sky to the upper right of the sun. It was truly a
magnificent spectacle: in broad daylight, a cluster of "stars" in a small
sector of the western sky were set against the backdrop of the deep
blue sky, flashing dazzling white light, constantly moving, constantly
forming all kinds of patterns. Especially around sunset, the sight of
the stars flashing, blue sky in the background, pink clouds below
reflecting them, was extraordinarily enchanting; the kind of sight one
would only expect in a dream!

'The number of "stars" kept changing: every few minutes we
counted now sixteen, now eighteen, twenty-two, twenty-six, twenty-
eight, twenty-nine, thirty-one, and thirty-two. The longest-lasting
number was thirty-two, and we weren't sure how it popped up. By
around 9.00 p.m., the number decreased. When they were disappearing most rapidly, there were still sixteen left.'

Six more witnesses wrote letters about this phenomenon to the *Journal
of UFO Research*. One of these, Kai Guohua, reported:

'At 8.00 p.m. on 7 July, just after the sun had set, its fading glow
spread an orange hue across the western sky. In that long stretch of
time while the sky was slowly turning from orange to blue, about
fifteen or thirty brilliant gold "stars" were hovering, and lined up in a
strange spidery design! Even though night had not yet fallen, the stars
were as bright as distant electric lights in the middle of the night.

'Before this, at 7.40 p.m., as the sun was setting, some people saw a
group of "stars" moving upwards and then gradually spreading apart.
There was a total of thirty-two of them, and they were lined up in
strange patterns. At the time I observed them, there were only
twenty-two left.'

This UFO event of 7 July was seen by a huge number of people in
China's Anhui, Jiangsu and Shandong Provinces, and caused a sensation. It was called 'an incredibly beautiful and rare phenomenon'.

Shawan District, Sichuan Province

The First Observation
The *Journal of UFO Research* received an interesting report by Song
Liang from China's Sichuan Province, describing sightings on 9 July
1990:

'The home of the teacher Liang Yingxiong of Jia Village, Shawan District, is in the Shawan District Chengxi Group Department of Industry Residence, fourth floor. Before daybreak on 9 July 1990, Yang Xuan, Ai Xianfu, and I went to his home to view that day's pre-dawn live broadcast of the 14th World Cup soccer games on China Central Television Network. To relax in the cool of the early hour, I went with Ai Xianfu and Liang Yingxiong to the balcony. After a few minutes, we happened to look at the sky, and there was not a star to be seen – no moon or light at all – it was pitch dark. But within seconds, Ai Xianfu caught sight of a disk-shaped blob of light which had suddenly appeared to the upper left of us (in the south-east). The following is what we saw before our eyes:

'When I first saw the flying saucer, its diameter was about 12 centimetres and it appeared to be a round blob of light, but not too distinct. As the blob of light gradually grew larger, to the point where its diameter was about 30 centimetres, its form became clear. It looked like two Chinese-style conical straw hats joined together, but not bulging out quite as much as the crown of a straw hat.

'Next, the flying saucer, maintaining a diameter of 30 centimetres and spiralling counter-clockwise, flew downwards and forwards toward the place from where we were watching it. It was noiseless and unblinking, and judging by appearances its speed would not have seemed very high, but considering its initial and final positions, it was going at an astonishing speed. After the approximately 30 seconds in which that occurred, the flying saucer suddenly stopped moving and shot out a sweeping flash of light. The flash of light was about 10 centimetres wide.

'At this time I rushed into the room from the balcony and shouted to Yang Xuan, then resting on the bed, to come and watch with us. When we reached the balcony, the flying saucer had ceased flashing its light, and continued approaching and descending in a counter-clockwise loop. This continued for about a minute. Suddenly, the saucer very quickly (in the blink of an eye) divided into two saucers about 60 centimetres apart. All the characteristics of the two saucers after the division – size, shape and brightness – seemed exactly the same as the one saucer before it split in two. The splitting took place while the saucer was moving but not flashing.

'The two saucers produced by the division continued approaching and descending in the same manner as before, and also gradually approached each other and combined into one. The joining also took place while the saucers were moving. In the process, the saucer grew to about 75 centimetres and began descending at a more rapid pace than before. It was no longer spiralling counter-clockwise and was now moving along a diagonal path. However, as it approached our position, it became fuzzy, faded and then suddenly disappeared. Then the whole sky returned to the dusky hue it had before the sighting. The entire observation lasted for about two minutes, from appearance to disappearance.'

The Second Observation
'After seeing the flying saucer, the four of us were quite excited. We all hoped that it would appear before us once again, and closer, so that we could observe it more clearly and determine its size, structure and whether or not it had a crew; and if so, whether or not the crew could communicate mentally with us, and so on. For this reason, the four of us kept watching the pre-dawn sky.

'After nearly two minutes, Yang Xuan was the first to see a blob of light suddenly appear to the south-east, but further south and a little closer to us than the first time. Its diameter was about 28 centimetres, and it had a tail with a very clear comet-tail form. This saucer must have been a bit brighter than the first one, and its pattern of motion was similar to that of the first saucer after recombining, but judging by its initial and final positions, it was not as fast as the saucer we witnessed in the first encounter.

'After about thirty seconds of this, the saucer suddenly stopped moving and shot out a sweeping light, which was about 60 centimetres wide. After the flash, the saucer suddenly disappeared. We didn't notice any fuzziness or fading before its disappearance. After it disappeared, the sky returned to its previous duskiness.'

Shanghai

Shanghai is the second largest city in the world, and with its population of 12 million is comparable to a small nation. Here, too, UFOs appear from time to time: indeed, they caused an uproar several times. There were three reported incidents in Shanghai in 1990, two of which will be described here.

11 January 1990
The first incident was reported to me by a junior high-school student named Zhao Gang:

'On the morning of the eleventh day of January 1990, the early bus from Baoshan to Nanmen was travelling south. It was still dark, and

53

the sky was full of stars. The bus driver suddenly noticed a peculiar luminous object right in front of the bus and about 300 metres above ground level. The object was about as high as a six-storey building. From its lower part a light flared which lit up a tree and lawn by the side of the road. The area it lit up was tremendously intense – as bright as daytime.

'This frightened the bus driver, and he stopped the bus. The passengers crowded to the windows and stuck their heads out to see. Suddenly, the object began approaching the bus. This reminded the driver of stories of flying saucers abducting people, and he was trembling with fear. But the object stopped in mid-air and after a few seconds began moving back faster and faster, then disappeared in the vastness of the night.'

The credibility of this story was enhanced when it was reported in a broadcast on Shanghai Radio.

31 October 1990
Lu Chenming, a resident of Shanghai, wrote a report for the *Journal of UFO Research* reviewing and analysing the following incident from start to finish:

'At 5.00 p.m. on 31 October 1990, on a day of perfectly fine weather in Shanghai in a clear blue sky,' he reported, 'a glowing unidentified flying object appeared in the northwestern sky flying in a northerly direction. Some witnesses said it was a flying saucer, others said it was the trail of an airplane. For this reason, the Shanghai Association for UFO Research held a "31 October UFO Analysis Session" on 9 December in the Putuo District Education Institute. I had the good fortune to attend this session and to see a replay of the shape and motions of the UFO on the videos, recorded on the spot by the Institute as well as Baoshan Television Station. Along with many others who attended the session, I believe it was a UFO, not an airplane trail.

'First of all, the glowing belt of the UFO did not look like an airplane trail. It was orange and extremely bright, and it had a bright spot in front. Concerning its shape, the videotape by the Educational Institute showed a short, thick, wide U-shape, and the video by Baoshan TV showed a dragon-tail shape, thick at the front and tapering off at the back. In contrast, the trail of an airplane (commonly called the contrail) does not glow [unless illuminated by the sun when low to or below the horizon – Ed.], and its form is dissimilar,

54

Plate 1.1. George Wingfield (centre), with Ralph Noyes (right) and Leslie Banks (left), who flies us over the cropfield formations each year. (© Timothy Good)

Plate 1.2. Part of the giant quadruple-ring Circle with four satellites (right) which appeared near Morgan's Hill, Devizes, Wiltshire, on 1 June 1990. A second formation appeared on 5 July 1990, and can be seen at the left, its ring intersecting the outer ring of the earlier formation. (© Timothy Good)

Plate 1.3. 'Insectogram' and another ringed formation at Stonehenge (in the background), 14 July 1991. (© George Wingfield)

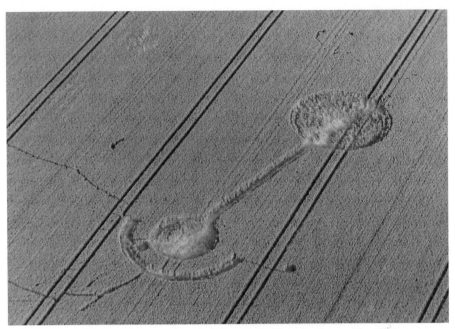

Plate 1.4. Dumb-bell pictogram with half-ring, discovered near East Kennett, Wiltshire, on 29 June 1991. (© George Wingfield)

Plate 1.5. The Alton Barnes pictogram, 2 July 1991. (© George Wingfield)

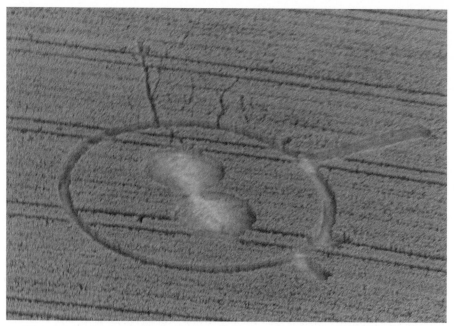

Plate 1.6. A pictogram which appeared at Ogbourne Maizey, near Marlborough, Wiltshire, on 11 July 1991. (© George Wingfield)

Plate 1.7. Pictogram near Hackpen Hill White Horse, Wiltshire, discovered on 12 July 1991. (© George Wingfield)

Plate 1.8. The Barbury Castle Pictogram, 17 July 1991. (© George Wingfield)

Plate 2.1. Chris Rutkowski standing in the centre of a Crop Circle near St Francois Xavier, Manitoba, in August 1990. (© Roy Bauer)

Plate 3.1. The FBI headquarters, Washington D.C. (© Timothy Good)

Plate 3.2. The National Security Agency headquarters at Fort Meade, Maryland.
(© Timothy Good)

Plate 4.1. Paul Dong (centre) after giving a lecture on UFOs at Ching Hua University, Beijing.

Plate 4.2. A meeting of the China UFO Research Organization.

Plate 5.1. Dr Richard Haines (at head of table) addresses members of the 'Expert Group on Anomalous Phenomena' at the USSR Academy of Sciences Building in Moscow, 12 February 1991.

Plate 6.1. Nikolai Lebedev, Leningrad, January 1989. (© Timothy Good)

normally dissipating out from a line; thin at the front and thick at the back, and there are usually ripple puffs. As for its speed, the UFO was moving slowly, and its tail exhibited a certain spiralling, while the trail of an airplane moves quickly and does not spiral.

'Secondly, there was no flight taking place at that time at the altitude of the trail. The aviation fuels used by airplanes are carbon oxides: they produce a great deal of moisture in the wake of the flight. If the temperature of the air is comparatively low ($-40C$ or below) and the humidity is comparatively high, then when the exhaust of the plane mixes with the surrounding air, it will condense into a contrail. Yet the humidity decreases with altitude, and according to the forecast for that day by the Army Weather Bureau, the altitude for contrails was 9,000–11,000 metres. If an airplane had been flying at that altitude, it would have left a trail, normally lasting about 30–40 seconds. Or, if a plane were approaching the bottom of the contrail altitude, its exhaust would expand with the cold, and as it rose to the condensation point it would also leave a trail. But the UFO was a moving belt of light, and it didn't linger in the air.

'Furthermore, in the period from 5.00 p.m. to 5.20 p.m., there was no flight activity by the air force, and there were only a few civil aircraft taking off and landing at Hongqiao Airport, all flying at very low altitude and thus unable to leave contrails. There was only one regularly scheduled Japan Air Lines Boeing 747 flying at 11,000 metres, which passed about 10 kilometres south of Shanghai, but even though the time matched, the JAL plane was flying from east to west with a northerly tendency, at an orientation of less than 45 degrees from the metropolitan area, meaning that its direction of flight did not match the south to north motion of the UFO; nor was its orientation the same.

'Also, because the JAL plane was flying at the upper boundary of the contrail altitude given in the forecast, it had no trail. Even if it had, a four-engined Boeing 747 would have been expected to have four very thick contrails, not like the U-shaped dragon-tail figure of the luminous belt.

'Furthermore, the UFO was not known to air traffic control. Under the Air Traffic Control Agency regulations, all flights passing into Shanghai must give advance notice to this agency. The agency confirmed that from 5.00 p.m. to 5.20 p.m. that day there were only six regularly scheduled civil aircraft in flight. Three of them – one bound for Tianjin, one for Xi'an and one for Beijing – were flying west past Wuxi on the way to their destinations, at an altitude of under 2,000 metres at the time they left Shanghai. Two other planes were arriving at Shanghai from Guangzhou and Beijing, flying east and also passing Wuxi before coming in to land at Hongqiao Airport. Their altitude at the time they entered Shanghai was 1,500–2,000 metres. The other plane was the JAL flight mentioned earlier.

'The Air Traffic Control Agency not only had these planes under close supervision, they could see them all clearly on their radar screens, and none had permission to enter Shanghai's restricted air-space. They didn't detect the slightest sign of a contrail flying from south to north. Only one target – the UFO hovering high above and flying slowly – failed to give advance notice to the agency, and not only flew from south to north across the north-west corner of the restricted Shanghai airspace, but also failed to reflect any signals to the radar screens of the air traffic controllers. And afterwards, the agency failed to hear of any mis-navigation or to receive any flight communications to fill in the gap.

'In conclusion, no matter how one looks at it – whether the glowing belt, the shape, the condensation trail altitude, or the air traffic control situation – there is no way the UFO of 31 October could have been a condensation trail left by an airplane.'

Because of the number of sightings in China in 1990, some psychics predicted that there would be even more in 1991.

Airliner Chases UFO over Shanghai
At 6.05 p.m. on 18 March 1991, Flight No. 5556 took off from Shanghai's Hongqiao Airport bound for Jinan, the capital of Shandong Province, some 800 kilometres to the north. At 6.13 p.m. Jin Xing, a controller from the Hongqiao Airport Control Centre, observed an elliptical ring of 'apricot-pink' light at an altitude of about 3,000 metres, near the airliner, and immediately radioed Mr Zhu, captain of the airliner.

Captain Zhu observed the UFO and began to follow it. He reported to the Control Centre that he saw an object, spurting a bright red blaze of light from its tail, and moving very quickly within the ring of light. Captain Zhu, piloting a British-built twin-turboprop Shorts 360–300 with thirty-six passengers on board, decided to give chase.

As the airliner flew over Kunshan, a small city about 60 kilometres north-west of Shanghai, the colour of the ring changed from orange to black, and two smaller objects separated from the ring. One of these objects was circular and the other rectangular. The two objects flew to and fro, maintaining a distance of 300 metres from each other.

Forty kilometres further on, the two objects suddenly turned toward the plane at high speed. Frightened, Captain Zhu asked the Control Centre for emergency help, at which point the two objects joined together and flew upwards rapidly.

Flight 5556 chased the UFO for a total of nine minutes. Captain Zhu, an experienced pilot, reported that there were no clouds in the sky and that visibility was excellent. The oval or circular object was larger than his plane, he said. No other aircraft were in the vicinity at the time of this alarming experience.

Airliner Encounter over Sichuan

According to the *Cheng Du Evening News* (20 May 1991), Southwest Airlines Flight No. 2408, en route from Cheng Du, Sichuan Province, to Sha Men, Fujian Province, encountered a UFO above Ji Yong city, about 260 miles from Cheng Du, on 17 May 1991.

At about 10.00 p.m. the crew of the Boeing 707 suddenly noticed a large, round, silver-coloured object to the right of the plane. As a safety precaution, the pilot tried to escape from the object by descending and turning off all lights. Four minutes later, the object went up into the clouds and disappeared. The UFO was also witnessed by the crew of Flight No. 154.

Finally, I would like to mention that thousands attending an official celebration in Sichuan Province saw 'a UFO slowly spinning through the night sky' on the same date. The UFO was sighted over the Tibetan district of western Xiancheng during a night rally held to mark the fifty-fifth anniversary of the Red Army's passage through the region during the 1934–35 Long March. I hope to provide further details in the next *UFO Report*.

Editor's Note

I am grateful to Professor Xie Chu, Editor-in-Chief of *Aerospace Knowledge*, for supplying me with an article on the Flight 5556 encounter, at the request of Paul Dong. *Aerospace Knowledge* is published by the Chinese Society of Aeronautics & Astronautics, 100083 Beijing, People's Republic of China.

5

A Scientific Research Trip to the Soviet Union

RICHARD HAINES

A well-known research scientist, Dr Richard F. Haines has three degrees in psychology from the Pacific Lutheran College, Tacoma, Washington and Michigan State University, and a degree in engineering from the University of Washington, Seattle, as well as an FAA Pilot Ground School Certificate. His past employment includes posts with the Boeing Airplane Co. and at NASA's Ames Research Center, where he has served as Chief of the Space Human Factors Office and as a research scientist, Life Sciences Division, as well as for the Research Institute for Advanced Computer Science, where he is currently employed.

Dr Haines has directed focused human vision research for the manned space programme in such areas as rendezvous/docking for the Gemini programme, spacecraft window design for the Space Station Freedom programme, and 'visual cue extraction from the real world' during landing by pilots of commercial aircraft. In 1989 he was appointed Project Manager for NASA's Remote Coaching Facility, which he helped design and develop. This facility is engaged in defining teleoperational concepts, transmission bandwidth requirements, and other telescience needs for carrying out future scientific operations on the Space Station Freedom.

Dr Haines's patents include designs for a visual examination apparatus, a simulator scene display evaluation device and a personal grooming device for microgravity. He is the author of over fifty-five articles in scientific journals and has produced three NASA technical films. He has edited *UFO Phenomena and the Behavioral Scientist* (1979) and is the author of *Observing UFOs* (1980); *Melbourne Episode – Case Study of a Missing Pilot* (1987); and *Advanced Aerial Devices Reported During the Korean War* (1990).

Dr Haines is currently researching material for a book on UFO sightings during the Vietnam War. He can be contacted at: PO Box 880, Los Altos, California 94023–0880.

In February 1991 I had the opportunity to meet a number of Soviet scientists in both Moscow and Novosibirsk and to discuss a variety of UFO-related topics as well as to carry out a detailed interview and hypnotic regression session with a UFO witness. This report summarizes these experiences.

On 18 February 1991, in Moscow, I met Dr Vladimir Rubtsov[1] of the Kharkov Engineering and Pedagogical Institute, Kharkov. He had arranged for me to meet with the 'Expert Group on Anomalous Phenomena' of the Soviet Academy of Sciences that afternoon to discuss current UFO events in America and the Soviet Union.

I first met Dr Yulii Platov of the Institute of Terrestrial Magnetism, Ionosphere and Radio Wave Propagation prior to arriving at the ultramodern Academy of Sciences building south of the city centre. Also present at this meeting were: Drs Alexander A. Panov, Geophysics Institute, Commission on Ecological Problems-Devices Department; Valery Miliaev, Vice-Director of the General Physics Institute and Director of the Tarusa GPI Branch; V. Feschin, Scientific-Technical Institute; V. Sokolov, Centre of Programme Research; G. Kulikova, IZMIRAN; V. Klepikov, IZMIRAN; and Sergei Chernouss, Head of Laboratory, Polar Geophysical Institute. The head of this group, Dr V. V. Migulin, corresponding member of the USSR Academy of Sciences, could not be present.

I had the privilege of reviewing my ongoing pilot sightings research with special emphasis upon the electromagnetic effects and statistical findings, as well as various photographic cases in which I had been involved. This was followed by my 35 mm slide presentation on photographic and CEII (Close Encounters of the Second Kind) evidence, which elicited a great deal of discussion. It was obvious that the scientists were unaware of this evidence but that it seemed to correspond in large degree with data they had collected.

The Soviet Scene

There has been a great deal of UFO activity in the Soviet Union over the past years. Some of these events have been documented by Dr Felix Zigel [of the Moscow Aviation Institute, who died in 1988 – Ed.] in his series of six volumes of typed reports. I was most fortunate to obtain a bound set of these volumes from Dr Sergei Bozhich, an applied mathematician. They are:

Vol. 1 *Nablydeneya NLO B CCCP* (UFO Observations in the USSR); No. 1, Moscow 1968 (200 pp).
Vol. 2 *Nablydeneya NLO B CCCP;* No. 2, Moscow 1975 (98pp)
Vol. 3 *Nablydeneya NLO B CCCP;* No. 3, Moscow 1978 (229pp).
Vol. 4 *Fenomen NLO B 1978 Gody* (UFO Phenomena in 1978); Moscow 1979 (233pp).

Vol. 5   *Posadke NLO B CCCP U Drygek Stranax* (UFO Landings in
the USSR and Other Nations); 1979 (212pp).
Vol. 6   *Petrozavodskoye Devo – 20 Centyabrya 1977 Goda*
(Petrozavodsk Events of 20 September 1977); Moscow 1980
(212pp).

Other more recent sightings are being documented in a new publication
Anomaleya (Anomalies),[2] edited by Sergei F. Bulantsev.[3] Issue 1 was
released in Moscow in January 1991 and consists of thirty-two (5.5. in-
×8 in) pages with clearly typeset text. This issue contains brief descriptions and discussions of sightings on 22 November 1989; 3 August 1990
at 23.45 hours local time in Kirov Region; 3 August 1990 in Tversk
Region; 18 and 19 August 1990 in Uzbekistan; 31 July 1989 at 21.03
hours local time in Dnepropetrovsk; 5 January 1989 at 17.00 hours local
time in Kazakhstan; 26 July 1990; 22 June 1990 at night in Kazakhstan;
and four black-and-white photos (February 1990 of lens flare; 21 March
1990 from the Ukraine; 3 February 1985 from Yalta; and 15 October
1968 from the Kolskii Peninsula).

Another new publication is a newspaper entitled *NLO Ekspress*
(UFO Express). Issue 1 was published in Novosibirsk in January 1991
and consisted of twenty-four (8 in×12 in)) pages.

An interesting article published in the 31 March 1990 issue of *Vecher-
nyaya Moskva* (Moscow Evening News), page 4, is entitled *Metamor-
fozi* (Metamorphosis) and reviews a sighting of 23–4 February 1990 in
Odessa. Sixteen separate phases of appearance were described in draw-
ings and in the text. I collected newspaper clippings for more than a
dozen other sightings.

Novosibirsk

I spent a week in Novosibirsk lecturing at the State University, the
Electrotechnical Institute and elsewhere. During this time I met the
following Ufologists: Evgenii V. Vorozhtsov, Institute of Theoretical
and Applied Mechanics of the USSR Siberian Division (Academy of
Sciences); Evgenii E. Vityaev, Institute of Mathematics; and B. Yu.
Scobelev, Institute of Theoretical and Applied Mechanics. They have
developed an interesting computer algorithm[4] which performs detailed
extraction of most of the available information in each UFO report.
Forty different features of the sighting are coded within a series of
phases, each phase consisting of a given flight dynamic.

There is a small but serious UFO study group in Novosibirsk consisting of about thirty persons, ten of whom play a central and continuing

role. They formed their group in 1978 as a result of receiving so many letters from people who had seen strange aerial phenomena. Almost none of the university scientists wanted to study these reports, so a small specialist group was formed (initially) to carry out correspondence with eyewitnesses and other investigators. Drs Zigel, Kuzofkin, Proetski, Migulin and others visited Novosibirsk over the years.

I spoke with Drs Svengenii Zhibizov, Victor Zhuravliev, and Alekseii Dmitriev of the State University, each of whom was deeply involved in field research in this region. Dr Dmitriev told me about one of his own sightings which took place at night in 1976 during a field expedition on geomagnetic characteristics of the Earth. Another member in his party took six consecutive photographs of the chevron-shaped lighted object. Although the photographer said he centred the light in the camera's viewfinder, after development the object's image was found to be displaced laterally about 30 degrees arc, for no apparent reason. Others using two additional cameras also obtained photographic images of the object. They noted fluctuations in the local magnetic field when the object was hovering nearby, and no such variations were noted at another sensor site 140 kilometres away. The variations lasted 14 minutes and the light was seen by nine witnesses. This case was never written up.

A Pilot's Close Encounters

I also met Vladimir Kuzmin, a jet pilot instructor who has flown for thirteen years and who has had several unusual sightings. He flew to Novosibirsk from Chelabinsk to tell me his stories. One of these events took place on 24 or 25 December 1989, while he was flying alone in an L-29[5] about 48 kilometres south of the centre of Chelabinsk.

While flying at an altitude of 8,000 metres, making various aerobatic manoeuvres, he noticed a yellow-white cigar-shaped object to the north of him at an estimated distance of 18–25 kilometres and an estimated altitude of 7,500 metres. It subtended an angle of about 5 degrees arc and remained horizontal and stationary. After performing a vertical loop where he could once again observe its direction, it had disappeared from view. He radioed to the air controller at the local airfield but they had nothing on radar except his own plane.

Our careful reconstruction of the event established that Kuzmin looked at the object for a total of about 4 minutes. Some time after he landed he noticed that his exposed facial region was covered with a thick crust which was sensitive (but not painful) to the touch. It was similar to a skin scald and was red. This gradually subsided and was gone after about ten to twelve days.[6] No nausea, dizziness or other physiological effects were noted after the sighting. He did not report the incident to the authorities.

Sometime later, Vladimir Kuzmin admitted that he had also seen a very strange silent light in the night sky while camping out with several friends. The event took place in autumn 1979 near the town of Oktoberskaya. All he could recall was watching a dark aerial body (with several dim lights across its equator) move smoothly towards them just above the treetops. It emitted a very intense, strangely shaped cone of white light shining down. The circle of light was brighter than daylight (white or light yellow) and estimated to be about 100 metres away from them. Its diameter was about 2–3 acres in area. They were all paralysed but could move their heads and eyes. The object and its beam stopped for a moment and then continued on out of sight.

When I heard that temporal discontinuity might be involved in his experience I felt that it might be worthwhile to use time-regression hypnosis to explore the witness's unconscious recall of this event. While I began the trance induction in Russian, I had to transfer the detailed instructions to a native, who spoke on my behalf in a calm and controll- ed tone of voice. We succeeded in achieving a deep trance relatively quickly in Mr Kuzmin, and a great deal of valuable additional informa- tion was obtained via the translator. My pre-hypnotic induction instruc- tions emphasized listening only to the translator's voice and not to mine. I will report the details of this case in a future publication.

Summary

In summary, I discovered that much the same UFO activities are taking place in these two areas of the Soviet Union as are occurring in America. I found that there are relatively more highly trained physical scientists studying unidentified aerial phenomena in the Soviet Union, and also that their peers often deride them for their efforts. They fund their efforts 'out of pocket', as we do, and do not have very many places to publish their work. We in the West should begin to share our data with them whenever possible.

REFERENCES
1. I first met Dr Vladimir V. Rubtsov on 12 November 1988 at the First International UFO Congress of Brussels. He is the author (with A. D. Ursul) of *Problems of Extraterrestrial Civilizations: Philosophical and Methodological Aspects* (1987).

2. Editorial office: 103009 Moscow, Tsentr, Tverkoy Blvd. 10–12, TACC, GRUU (USSR).
3. Mr Bulantsev took part in the nationally televised show *UFO Cover-up? Live* in October 1988, broadcast from Washington D.C.
4. Part of this algorithm is based on work reported in an Academy of Science Technical Report, No. 002, entitled *Premeneneye Teoree Invariantnik Mnogoobrazee v Methode Parametricheskoy Korrektsee Raznostnix Schem*, Institute of Automatic Design, 1990 (26pp).
5. The L-29 Delfin is a two-place jet trainer manufactured in Czechoslovakia. [*Editor's note:* It is more likely that the aircraft involved in this incident was the single-seat aerobatic version, designated the L-29 Akrobat.]
6. This airplane had a plexiglass canopy which blocks a very large percentage of ultraviolet (UV) radiation. UV wavelengths are those which are shown to cause sunburn. Either the UFO emitted very high level of UV radiation or the skin crust which formed was due to an entirely different physiological response mechanism. It was probably not microwave radiation, since no permanent tissue damage or pain was experienced.

6

The Soviet Scene 1990

NIKOLAI LEBEDEV

The son of an air force pilot, Nikolai Lebedev was born in Valday, USSR, in 1950. He studied at the Institute of Mechanical Engineering in Leningrad from 1968 to 1975, at the same time studying developments in aeronautics and astronautics. He now specializes in irrigation engineering and lives with his wife and small son in Leningrad, where I first met him in 1989. His interest in UFOs was stimulated in 1983, when he read a book about unexplained mysteries by Helmut Höflung.

In December 1990 Nikolai Lebedev visited London and shared a great deal of information with me, some of which is included in the following article. Additional Soviet military reports from 1990 (also supplied to me by Nikolai) can be read in my book, *Alien Liaison: The Ultimate Secret* (Century, London 1991).

'The phenomenon of UFOs is real and we should approach it seriously and study it.'

Thus did President Mikhail Gorbachev reply to a question during a meeting with workers in the Urals district in April 1990, as reported in *Soviet Youth.*[1] Tremendous interest in the subject is shown by the public and many sightings of UFOs have been reported in the Soviet Union during 1990.

A Landing in Estonia

On the evening of 23 March 1990, E. Pavlov, an officer of the local garrison in the town of Kohtla-Iarve, Estonia, went out on to the balcony of his house and was startled by the appearance of a silent, disc-shaped object in the sky, with bright yellow lights along its perimeter.

Together with his wife, Pavlov observed the object descending and hovering about 1.5 metres from the ground, near the electricity substation, at a distance of about 150 metres from them. Pavlov fetched his binoculars and determined that the object was about 15 metres in diameter and 3–7 metres in height. Apparently, some children then attempted to get close to the object and it flew away in the direction of Leningrad.

On 27 March, the same or similar object appeared at the same time in the evening and landed near the substation. On this occasion, Pavlov managed to take photographs, one of which is reproduced here (Fig. 6:1). Sadly, this is reproduced from a newspaper, as I have been unable to obtain a print at the time of writing. The photographs are being analysed by experts from the Estonian Commission on Anomalous Phenomena.

Figure 6:1.

The flying saucer returned yet again on the following night (28 March), and was observed by hundreds of people, including a correspondent from *Rabochaya Tribuna* (Workers' Tribune), E. Kapov.[2]

Extraterrestrials at Kairma?

It was 18 May 1990. In the village of Kairma, near Frunze, Kirgizskaya, the day was not too warm and there were no signs of a storm which began in the evening. At 21.40 hours, when the rain had nearly stopped, Dima, a 10-year-old boy, ran outside his home then suddenly returned, with a look of horror on his face.

'Mother,' he cried, 'extraterrestrials are here!'

Taking her son by the hand, the mother went outside and she, too, saw the beings. 'I have never seen such creatures before,' she said. 'They wore helmets and their height was about 1.1 metres. They wore suits with stripes on their sleeves and trouser legs.'

Dima added that the being had hands with three fingers, as sharp as claws, and that their suits were glowing. He also reported that when they noticed him, they pulled out a box-like device from behind them and some things like aerials appeared on their heads. Their footsteps were very light, almost as if they were sliding.

Beside the house there is a ditch with water. When a car appeared from the distance, all the beings jumped into the ditch and remained under the water until the car had passed by! Dima's mother said that the air all around them was vibrating. They were both frightened and ran to a neighbour's house, but when they came out into the street there was no sign of the creatures. The mother and her son observed the beings for about 10 minutes.

When Dima later showed a research team the place where the beings were 'walking', they noticed that the grass was depressed and had become yellow. In his letter to me, M. S. Eltsin reported that when members of his team stood in the area, their legs became strangely numb.

At 23.30 a strong droning sound was heard over Kairma, and voltage in the electrical transmission system began to fluctuate markedly. Showers of sparks could be seen falling from the substation. Later, the electricity supply cut out altogether. A local electrical engineer as well as an engineer from Frunze were unable to find any signs of damage.

At about 00.30 on 19 May, a huge red disc-shaped object flew over Kairma, with bright white beams of light coming down from it.

By morning, the voltage had returned to normal. At 13.21, a whole group of UFOs, resembling grey-coloured discs, were seen flying very fast from south to east, over the central part of Frunze. Many eyewitnesses reported this sighting, one of them a member of the Kirgizskaya research team.

On 21 May, nine strange 'dots' appeared in the sky over Kairma, flying at great speed over a field. They seemed to be flying in some kind of order – in threes – and not far from them could be seen a large red disc-shaped 'cloud'.

On 29 May, 3 kilometres from the place where the creatures had been seen, the most astonishing incident occurred at a garage on a collective farm. At the beginning of the working day (08.50), there are usually many drivers in the area, but at this particular time there were none. In the control office were three women: T. M. Knaup, Ludmila Sadovskaia and a trained nurse, A. L. Sitnik.

Suddenly, strange 'horn-like' sounds could be heard, becoming stronger, followed by the sensation of a 'presence'. Ludmila raised her head and through the window of the office she saw a strange creature, with something glowing where the eyes should be. [Compare with the Puerto Rico encounter described in Chapter 8 – Ed.] She also noticed an absence of nose and a slit for the mouth. The face was greenish-grey in colour.

Ludmila told Knaup to lock the door, and at this moment the sound of footsteps could be heard moving away. All attempts to ask for assistance by radio were in vain. The three women then ran out of the office, shouting for assistance. No one else saw the creature who visited the building, but many drivers later reported seeing strange footmarks, as if from dust or powder. These later disappeared. The marks were about 30 mm in diameter, with three 'stripes'. The needle of a compass deviated up to 90 degrees where the creature had been 'standing', and the investigators noted a feeling in the ears similar to that experienced during change of altitude in a plane.

The secretary of the Party committee, V. P. Kazak, said that the women who reported the incident were all very serious, and not normally of a hysterical disposition.

There were eyewitnesses who observed this incident from another position. Two boys, living nearby, who were guiding cattle near the garage, saw a 'flying saucer' appear above the garage and land after a few manoeuvres. One of the boys was too frightened to stay and observe anything further, but 8-year-old Mashmich Artem approached the garage and hid behind a wheel. He observed how a hatch opened and a ladder was pulled out of the craft, following by seven 'pilots'.

Mashmich claimed that one of the beings was about 3 metres tall and the others were about a metre and a half, wearing bright golden-coloured, close-fitting overalls with emblems like human figures with wings. On the feet could be seen something like studs. The boy noticed two aerials on the head of the tall being, from which were spreading 'concentric circles'. The group then divided into two, and the first group began to collect mazut [blackoil] from the ground. Interestingly, this viscous liquid 'gathered' into a sphere, then appeared in the beings' hands. The second group headed for the office building and one 'pilot' approached the office itself.

Later, the boy saw the women running from the office. After 15 minutes, the beings returned to their craft which took off, then landed again not far from a repair shop.

Although there were drivers in the vicinity of the garage, no one reported to the women that they had seen either the craft or its pilots. The incident was investigated within hours, and in his report M. S. Eltsin informed me that the footmarks next to the garage were the same as those at Kairma, and that he experienced the same sensation of a change in atmospheric pressure.

It is the opinion of Eltsin and myself that the drivers in the vicinity of the garage were probably under the 'influence' of the beings, in much the same way as many witnesses to the landings at Voronezh [see *The UFO Report 1991* – Ed.] never spoke about their experience.

A Sighting by the Militia in Frunze

At about 17.30 on 21 September 1990, the Administrative Office of Interior Affairs at Frunze, Kirgizskaya, received a telephone call from the region of the so-called South Gate, located near the old airport. A huge UFO was said to be manouevring in that area.

Ten minutes later, a patrol car with three officers of the Militia arrived on the scene. They were: K. P. Kalugin, Duty Officer Responsible; T. A. Isakov, Head of Investigations Department; and S. I. Savoschin, a specialist in radio communications. Just after leaving the built-up area of the town, they saw a giant UFO, estimated in their official report to be 104 metres in diameter, hovering at a height of about 150 metres.

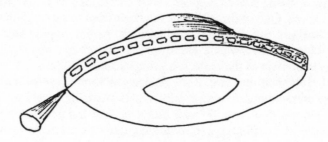

Figure 6:2.

From one side of the UFO a yellow cone-shaped beam of light could be seen, ending very sharply not far from the craft (Figure 6:2). Isakov took some photographs, but the sensitivity of the film was low (16 DIN), and they did not come out well. A cupola was seen very distinctly, as well as a row of glowing 'portholes' (?) on the rim, and another cupola could be seen underneath the craft. Periodically, light seemed to be rotating around the rim.

As if in response to the patrol car, the UFO began to move to the south, in the direction of Orto-Sai. The officers then lost track of the object, but observed it again as it moved over the hills on the outskirts of Orto-Sai. The UFO was flying away from them, but a strong glow could be seen coming from one of the hills. Getting out of the patrol car, the officers climbed up the hill, and observed the UFO, which remained for a while, leaving a large area of burning grass (Plate 6:2) in the form of a cross (Figure 6:3).

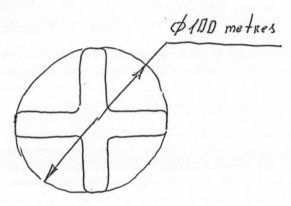

Figure 6:3.

The landing site was visited by A. P. Sidelnikov, a militia captain, who later informed researchers about the incident. The damaged area was about 100 metres in diameter, and 'honeycomb-like' imprints were also found. Information about the incident was later published in a Kirgizskaya newspaper.[3]

Whose Is The Skull?

During 1990 many inhabitants of Aramza, in the region of Susamyr, Kirgizskaya, reported strange, sphere-like objects in the sky, and many more people claimed to have seen a strange 'Bigfoot'- or 'Snowman'-type creature.

In October, shepherd Emil Akitaev was not too surprised when his dog carried in a bloodstained skull to his tent. However, the head veterinary surgeon of the pastures in that region, Mairambek Man-akulov, was certain that the skull (Plate 6:3) belonged to neither an animal nor a human being. The skull had a large cranium with a long nasal section, as well as a fixed joint which was attached to the skull where the neck vertebrae should join.

Manakulov delivered the skull to the Panfilovski Central Regional Hospital. According to the head physician, Sh. B. Begaliev, the skull could belong to a creature with a highly developed intellect, but of non-human origin. He based his opinion on the large volume of the cerebral hemispheres, and the fact that there were no normal eye sockets or nasal holes. In addition, the bone material contained a very low level of calcium.[4]

I am informed that this skull has been under investigation at a research institute in Moscow, and I hope to publish details in the next *UFO Report.*

On the subject of Bigfoot creatures, I have to say that, in my opinion, in most cases these relate to a type of extraterrestrial reconnaissance.

Night Encounter in Leningrad

It was around 1 a.m. on the night of 17 June 1990 when 42-year-old bus driver Aleksandr Pavlovich Dolotov came out of his relative's flat, not far from Leningrad's Baltiyski station. Shortly before, he had made a phone call to his wife Rita, who works as a doctor and was on duty at the station.

Dolotov was walking along Lermontovski Prospekt, near the Hotel Sovetskaia (Plate 6:4), and he could see the lights of the station. He thought it rather strange that the street was deserted. Going round an obstacle on the pavement he suddenly noticed four peculiar men, approaching him in pairs. They were 2 metres tall, with well-proportioned figures, wearing what looked like black diving-suits and black helmets, but with faces and hands exposed.

There was an unusual difference between the rate at which these men walked – which was very fast – and the actual movement of walking. When they were about 10 metres from Dolotov, he suddenly lost consciousness. Regaining consciousness, he found himself in the Volodarski Hospital, and the time was 05.00. He was told that he had been found near house no. 66 on Izmailovski Prospekt (Plate 6:5). After formal checking, he was allowed to go home. He contacted his wife (who had already been informed that he was in hospital) before going to meet her. While in hospital, he noticed some strange holes in his trousers, as if they had been cut out (Plate 6:6). The photos made later show edges that are slightly rough, but his wife confirms that they appeared initially as if they had just been cut.

At Baltiyski station Dolotov was met by his wife. 'What's the matter? What's happened?' she asked. 'I had a fight with soldiers,' he replied. Rita examined him and his clothes carefully. I must add that she is very skilled in these matters, as she is often asked to help the militia in incidents relating to fights. His clothes were indeed dirty in some places, but these were not the marks of a street fight. Furthermore, there were no signs of a violent struggle on his body, although she noticed two unusual wounds below the knee, which had already formed scars. Dolotova told me that the wounds were oval in shape, bloodless and clean. These were not wounds one would get in a street fight. Moreover, they did not coincide with the holes in the trousers as to shape and arrangement.

'What makes you think that you were beaten by soldiers?' asked Rita. This question perplexed Aleksandr. Under persistent questioning, he recalled the trip along the Lermontovski Prospekt and the meeting with strangers, and remembered another incident which may be significant. He recalled the men bending over him in black helmets, and that they told him: '*Remember, you were beaten by soldiers*'. He also recalls being told that it would be harmful for him to speak about the incident.

The situation regarding 'soldiers' became clearer when Rita Dolotova had spoken with Dr Olga Fedorovna Goriacheva, the doctor who was in the ambulance that took Aleksandr to the hospital. She told me (and at first her husband) that a phone call had been made to the medical station by a soldier, who explained that a man was lying on the Izmailovski Prospekt near house no. 66. At 01.55 an ambulance took Aleksandr away, arriving at the hospital at 02.15. Dr Goriacheva said that when they approached the house, they noticed that three soldiers were holding Aleksandr, trying to keep him upright. His eyes were open, but all attempts to find out what had happened to him were in vain. Without any connection to the questions, he kept repeating only one word: 'Never.'

'What was the diagnosis?' I asked Dr Goriacheva. She replied that in her opinion, Aleksandr Dolotova's condition was due to strong concussion, but it must be pointed out that this opinion was not arrived at as a result of careful medical examination: he had not even been undressed at the hospital. It should also be pointed out that the distance between the Lermontovski Prospekt and the Izmailovski Prospekt (where he was found) is more than 600 metres. My own opinion is that this incident was the result of action by 'Ufonauts'. What was behind this action, and where was the Ufonauts' craft during this operation?

All my attempts to gather additional information by means of a direct appeal in our Leningrad newspaper, *Vecherni Leningrad*, were in vain. I do not consider this incident as frightening. Perhaps many extraterrestrial civilizations are working on Earth, with different motives and methods of operation.

Air Force Interception of a UFO

In October 1990, *Rabochaya Tribuna* included an article on the pursuit of a UFO by an interceptor pilot, after S. Prokoshin, the commanding officer of an air force unit, reported that a blip designating an aerial target had suddenly appeared on radar screens near Tbilisi, Georgia at 11.00 on 8 October 1990. Here is the report by the pilot, Major P. Riabishev:

'At 11.22, I received the co-ordinates of the target and the mission to take a look at it . . . According to the information from the command post, the object was located at an altitude of 4.5 kilometres. The weather was clear and cloudless, the visibility excellent. But a search for the target did not yield any results. I reported this, turned, and headed home.

'Suddenly, something made me turn my head. To the rear and to the right, I saw two cigar-shaped objects of considerable dimension. The length of the first approximately two kilometres and the second about 400 metres. They were positioned one behind the other and were in good view against the background of a clear sky. The smaller one cast a silver colour in the rays of the sun and the larger one appeared to be lustreless. But I was not able to make out any details or structural features – the distance was too great. I noticed, in fact, the UFOs moving sideways at great speed.

'I turned and began to close in. And suddenly both targets disappeared from the field of vision. But the blips stayed on the radar. According to information from the command post, about 15 kilometres separated us at this point.'[5]

Sighting by Cosmonauts

Another issue of *Rabochaya Tribuna*, as well as *Soviet Youth*, contained an interview with cosmonauts aboard the space station Mir, by Leonid Lazarevich, a journalist who was communicating with the cosmonauts by radio. The interview, on 28 September, focused on an enormous UFO that they reportedly observed in space. The cosmonauts were G. M. Manakov and G. M. Strekalov:

L.L.:   Tell me, what are the most interesting natural phenomena you see on Earth?

G.M.: Yesterday, for example, I saw – if one may call it that – an unidentified flying object. I called it that.

L.L.: What was it?

G.M.: Well, I don't know. It was a great, silvery sphere, it was iridescent . . . this was at 22.50.

L.L.: This was over the region of Newfoundland?

G.M.: No. We had already passed over Newfoundland. There was an absolutely clean, clear sky. It is difficult to determine, but the object was at a great altitude over the Earth – perhaps 20–30 kilometres. It was much larger than a huge ship.

L.L.: Could it have been an iceberg?

G.M.: No. This object had a regular shape, but what it was, I don't know. Perhaps an enormous, experimental sphere, or something else . . .[6]
I was observing it for about six or seven seconds, then it disappeared.

L.L.: But is it possible for you to determine approximately its speed?

G.M.: It simply was hovering over the Earth . . .[7]

Radar/Visual Incident near Kuybyshev

The following event occurred at the long-range radar tracking station near Kuybyshev (now again called Samara), on 13 September 1990, beginning at 00.07. Major A. L. Duplin, head of the shift watch at the time, reported:

'At the beginning of the first hour, a large flying object was observed on the radar screen. The brightness of this blip was comparable to that of a strategic bomber approaching us, and the distance was no more than 100 kilometres.' (I should point out that this is a very powerful radar complex, and even small targets can be detected at greater distances.)

'Following my order, enquiries were made via the automatic identification system, but I was informed by Senior Sergeant Miketenok that this system had gone out of operation . . . At this moment, the "strategic bomber" target scattered, and changed into what looked like a flock of birds on the radar screen . . .'

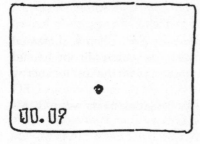

Figure 6:4.

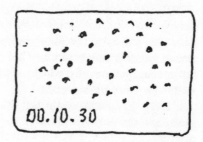

Figure 6.5

One explanation was that the multiple targets could have been caused by reflections generated by parts (such as boosters) from a rocket launch, but this theory was soon discounted, since at a distance of 42 kilometres the radar screen showed a strong signal from the main target, representing an isosceles triangle with flat sides. Another explanation was birds, but this was also discounted. 'To glow on the screen at such a distance, these "birds" must have had a plumage of steel with cobalt!' remarked Major Duplin. Moreover, a triangular UFO actually landed at the radar base! (Later, the military correspondent, Captain D. Rudzit, obtained permission via Air Defence Command to see a video-tape of the radar recordings.)

The target came much closer, and the underground command post ordered a team to investigate, headed by Captain Lazeiko, who repor-ted as follows:

'An unknown object passed over our heads as we came out of the underground bunker. Its height was no more than about 10 metres . . . We could see it clearly, since the perimeter of the base is always lit by searchlights. The bottom of the object was smooth, but not mirror-like – it was like a thick layer of soot. We did not notice any openings, portholes or landing gear, but we saw three whitish-blue beams of light. The corners of the object were slightly rounded.'

According to Senior Sergeant B. Gorin, the commander of the guard who was in the guardroom just after the relief of the guard, a sentry, Corporal A. Blazhis, could not be contacted at post No. 4. At 00.20, Gorin sent two soldiers to find out what had happened. In his report, one of the soldiers, Sergeant A. Romanov, explained that all the tele-phone equipment at the post was in perfect working order but there was no sign of Blazhis. On learning this, Gorin gave the order, 'To arms!', and organized a search for Blazhis. Half-an-hour later it was reported that he had disappeared, together with another sentry, A. Varenitsa.

'After the report [of the missing corporals],' said Major Duplin, 'I decided to scan the unidentified object, which had apparently landed near the fence by the short-range radar post [No. 12]. I had time to notice on the radar screen that just after the triangular object dis-appeared, sources of [radar] radiation could still be seen at the ends of where the triangle had been.'

Captain P. Lazeiko reported that as he ran up to post No. 12, he saw a flash, and the aerials appeared to be on fire, 'as if made of wood'. (The military correspondent, Captain Rudzit, said that he was not permitted to take photos at the site, but was shown the remains of the aerial.)

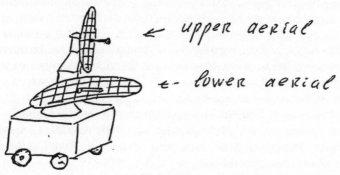

← upper aerial

← lower aerial

Figure 6:6.

Another witness to the landing, Corporal S. Dudnik, described the event as follows:

'I was standing on sentry duty at post No. 6 and saw the arrival of a large, black, triangular flying object, each side about fifteen metres in length. It landed from above – not too quickly – with a soft rustling sound. The thickness of the triangle was about three metres. The flash, which knocked down the aerial behind me, came from the centre of the side of the object. There were no openings that I could see, but it seemed to be aiming at the target, and I was directly in the

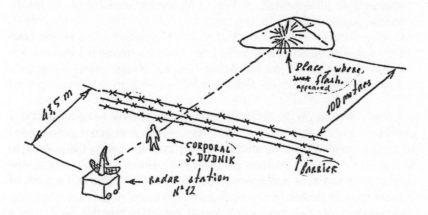

Figure 6:7.

75

firing line! Strangely, I did not come to any harm, but the aerial was knocked down and burned brightly.'

P. Beshmetov (rank-and-file) ran up to Corporal Dudnik when the fire started. 'He was standing near the barbed wire barrier with his tommy-gun directed to the large black triangle, which was 100 metres from the barbed wire. I prepared to shoot, too,' Beshmetov reported.

'The triangle took off after one and a half hours, and the commander of the guard ordered all the soldiers back to their posts and to check the barrier. The colour of the radar-truck before the flash was dark green, but afterwards its paint became black and blistered. Some parts of the truck had melted. The upper aerial had broken away and was lying on the ground, three metres away from the truck. All its steel parts had melted, with the exception of the aluminium dish itself. The officers told Captain Rudzit that the steel parts burned as if in a stream of oxygen, and they could not understand what sort of energy could have caused steel to burn from such a distance [143.5 metres from the UFO to radar post No. 12].

'When I came up to the storehouse, out came Corporal Blazhis. He was very surprised to see me walking along his post. I asked him where he had been for such a long time. He began to laugh, and said that as he was going to the phone to report to Sergeant Romanov, he suddenly lost his memory . . . Simultaneously, A. Varenitsa, the other missing sentry, also appeared at his post. He too remembered nothing, and is convinced that all the time he remained at the post. In his opinion, it was as if we all appeared to them in an instantaneous film – suddenly soldiers appeared with tommy-guns.

'The watches of corporals Blazhis and Varenitsa were one hour and fifty-seven minutes slow and one hour and forty minutes slow, respectively. In addition, the serial numbers of Blazhis' tommy-gun and bayonet were completely wiped out.'

In his report to the commander of the radar complex, the head of the economic managerial platoon, Boris Voronkov, demanded punishment of the two sentries for burning the aerial and destroying the vegetable patch (above which the UFO had hovered): obviously, he did not accept that a UFO had been responsible. The ground looked as if it had been subjected to an explosion of some kind. According to the observers, the object did not actually land, but hovered just above the ground.

The commander of the radar complex said that a special commission from the Ministry of Defence was due to visit the site on 18 September, five days after the incident.

Denial

The main newspapers reported these extraordinary events, as did the military newspaper *Za Rodinu*, a newspaper for the large and important Privolzhski–Uralski military district, and the article was reprinted in full in Irkutsk by the local *Soviet Youth*.[8]

But on 23 September 1990, the *Workers Tribune* published a story explaining that the deputy chief of *Za Rodinu* was ordered to visit the staff of military district commander General Makashov, and that the military correspondent D. Rudzit and his chief were now denying the incident. The following month, *Trud* published information from the headquarters of the military district that the story of a UFO landing at the radar complex was an invention by the military correspondent of *Za Rodinu*.[9]

Finally, all serious interest in the story was killed when General Tretiak, Deputy Minister of Defence and Commander-in-Chief of the Air Defence Forces (who also holds the position of General of the Army), gave an interview in *Literaturnaya Gazeta* in November 1990:

> Recently a report appeared in *Rabochaya Tribuna* that some kind of flying vehicle appeared in the Kuybyshev district, and, what is more, it destroyed our radar station. Naturally, we were perplexed – why was there no report? A destroyed radar station – it is a major incident. Even if it had been hit by lightning, it would have been necessary to report this immediately. And here we have an attack by a flying vehicle. But it can be explained. *Rabochaya Tribuna* took these reports from the district [military] newspaper, *Za Rodinu*. It turns out that the hoax was thought up by a staff member of the newspaper in order to attract readers. Maybe, right now, even as we speak, this captain is in the office of General Makashov and the latter is, as they say, flaying him alive . . .[10]

At the end of November 1990 I spoke with Emil Bachurin, leader of the UFO research group in Perm, Siberia. He told me that his close friend, Colonel X, was invited to the radar complex near Samara, not long after the visit from the Ministry of Defence commission (18 September). The colonel was informed that the upper aerial of radar post No. 12 and its instruments were taken away by the commission to be studied by the Scientific Research Department of the Ministry of Defence. He was personally shown the videotapes from the radar screen and the site where the incident had taken place. After having spoken with all the witnesses, the colonel concluded that the incident did indeed happen as initially reported.

In conclusion, I would again like to quote General Tretiak: 'To my mind, there is no evidence that unidentified flying objects which appear from time to time are extraterrestrial spacecraft. . . . There are no reasons for believing that even one spacecraft has flown over or landed in the territories of the Soviet Union. . . .'

As we can see, *glasnost* depends to a large extent on the attitude of our Ministry of Defence . . .

REFERENCES
1. *Soviet Youth*, 4 May 1990
2. *Rabochaya Tribuna*, 7 April 1990.
3. *Komsomolets Kirgizia*, 10 October 1990.
4. Ibid.
5. *Rabochaya Tribuna*, 20 October 1990.
6. *Soviet Youth*, 2 November 1990.
7. *Rabochaya Tribuna*, 16 October 1990.
8. *Soviet Youth*, 11 October 1990.
9. *Trud*, 5 October 1990.
10. *Literaturnaya Gazeta*, 7 November 1990.

Editor's Note

It might be helpful here to include some additional remarks made by the Soviet Deputy Defence Minister, General Ivan Tretiak, during the interview published in *Literaturnaya Gazeta* in November 1990.

Asked by columnist O. Moroz if the Air Defence Forces regard the flight of UFOs in Soviet airspace as a 'violation of the sovereignty of the USSR', Tretiak replied that it was premature to regard UFOs as a threat, because although the reports by pilots indicated that the UFOs appeared to be of artificial origin, their real nature had yet to be determined. Observing that most previous sightings had been explained as natural phenomena or as misinterpretations of optical phenomena associated with rocket launches or artificial debris that is congesting space near Earth, Tretiak added that: 'Many of the phenomena taken for UFOs are caused by the penetration of cosmic rays through ozone holes which are formed during [rocket] launches.' He revealed that the military knew that some of the famous UFO sightings in the late 1970s could have been explained by making this effect public knowledge, but that 'for security reasons, nothing was written about this at that time.'

Tretiak replied negatively when asked whether the Air Defence Forces had detected any of the UFOs cited in five sighting reports in 1990. As an example of multiple observations of a UFO – in this case by the Air Defence Forces – Tretiak cited an unidentified flying vehicle that was reported by his Chief of Staff, Colonel Maltsev, in March 1990 (see *Alien Liaison: The Ultimate Secret*). Tretiak stated that one UFO had been photographed, and optical and thermal signals from it had shown up on the target screens of the jet interceptors.

'For quite a long time – from 20.00–23.30 – in the region north-east of Moscow [Pereslavl–Zaleskii, Zagorsk, Fryazino, Kirzak],' said Tretiak, 'two pulsating lights were observed in the sky, moving as if they were fixed in position in relation to each other, like the side lights of an aircraft. But this was not an airplane. We have written testimony from eyewitnesses as well as photographs. Some observers were even convinced that the speed of the object depended on the frequency of pulsation of the lights.'

Tretiak noted that although the object could be observed on a radar screen and photographed, it could not be registered by onboard radar recording equipment. He explained that the 'three signals which come in from a target – the radar signal, the optical signal, and the thermal signal – all show up on the viewing screen. It is as if they duplicate each other, but the recording device only registers the radar signal. And, in this [21 March] case, there was none.' He said he believed that the UFO could not be recorded on radar because it was not an ordinary flying machine which can be recorded on the relatively narrow band on which Air Defence Forces radar operates.

The Deputy Defence Minister went on to explain that the UFO appeared to have 'stealth-like' characteristics. Expressing his hope that technological progress will make it possible to widen the capability of radars to counteract 'stealth' features, he said: 'It is known, for example, that there are a number of materials and shapes which sharply lower the radar and optical profile of an object . . . That is precisely what is being achieved in the American Stealth programme . . . I admit that the measures aimed at countering this programme, which we are now taking, will simultaneously promote the solution of the UFO riddle.' He suggested that 'if special observation posts were organized and the frequencies on which radars operate were expanded . . . we most likely would see more. For this, however, very great resources are necessary. The ground radars of the Air Defence Forces also did not record the [UFO] target.'

When asked why he, as Commander-in-Chief of the Air Defence Forces, did not order the UFO to be shot down, particularly since his predecessor in the post of Commander-in-Chief, as well as the Minister of Defence, had been removed from their positions when they were unable to prevent 'a flight over our territory and a landing in Moscow of the inoffensive sports plane flown by Rust', Tretiak pointed out that the UFOs encountered thus far by his pilots have appeared to pose no extraterrestrial threat and that there is still no proof that the UFOs are of extraterrestrial origin or flown by intelligent beings. Moreover, he warned, it would be foolhardy to launch an unprovoked attack against an object that may possess formidable capacities for retaliation.

Tretiak said that even if it is proven that some of the UFOs are 'a product of a highly organized intelligence from a significantly more developed civilization that our own . . . any fight with such objects and their crews – before a clarification of their intentions – would be futile . . .'

(I am indebted to Dr Bruce Maccabee for providing me with this information, which is contained in a Foreign Press Note, dated 2 January 1991, published by the CIA's Foreign Broadcast Information Service and obtained by Dr Maccabee from a source in the CIA's Science and Technology Center.)

7

Gulf Breeze: A Continuing Saga

BOB OECHSLER

Bob Oechsler interrupted his education at the University of Maryland to join the US Air Force in 1968, serving mostly with the American Forces Radio and Television Service in the continental United States. During the Vietnam War he served in Cambodia, Thailand and Laos, and some of his work during this period involved the filming of classified prototype weapons systems.

On returning to the US, Bob Oechsler spent a year and a half at Wright-Patterson AFB, then in 1972 left the Air Force and returned to the University of Maryland. He next joined NASA at the Goddard Space Flight Center in Greenbelt, Maryland, specializing in missions technical analysis as a prototype designer of sophisticated control systems and mobile surveillance systems. Among the projects he was involved in were the International Ultraviolet Explorer and the Apollo-Soyuz Test Project.

Bob is Assistant State Director of MUFON in Maryland, as well as Director of the Annapolis Research and Study Group. Since 1987 he has hosted a nationwide programme, *UFOs Today*, featuring interviews with key witnesses and researchers.

Bob's contacts with the US Intelligence Community have led to a wealth of sensational information pertaining to above top secret research into UFOs, which I published in *Alien Liaison: The Ultimate Secret* (Century, London 1991)

At the time when the first UFO sighting activity was sowing the seeds of change in the small peninsula town in north-west Florida known as Gulf Breeze, all of my spare time was occupied in the study of scientific analysis of UFO photographs and films.

Although I had had some experience with electronic satellite and data-compiled photographic mediums from my work in the astronomy laboratories at the University of Maryland and at NASA's Goddard Space Flight Center, my expertise in negative and print film was limited, and my experience with Polaroid film was non-existent. Thanks to the tutorial assistance of Ray Stanford, his extensive collection of UFO photographs and films, and his knowledge of applied physics, I was beginning to get the feel for his exceptional eye for detail. Although I was unable to see some of the extraordinary detail that Ray's keen eyes were capable of observing in the photographic evidence that he had personally acquired, the experience was rewarding and added a practical workshop-type atmosphere to the studies I had been conducting of the methodologies of Dr Richard Haines and Dr Bruce Maccabee.

Preliminary Investigation

I got my first taste of an actively evolving UFO photographic case at a meeting of the Fund for UFO Research in January 1988, when Dr Maccabee, a civilian optical physicist with the US Navy, obtained copies of the first five Polaroids taken by Ed Walters on 11 November 1987 in Gulf Breeze. What was truly unique about the case, however, was the video tape that was subsequently taken on 28 December 1987, clearly showing the same type of object in flight as had previously been photographed. The video tape particularly appealed to me because I still had access to a well-equipped video production and editing studio at the Goddard Space Flight Center, and I was certain of great interest there.

The Gulf Breeze case was unique right from the start, not only because of the existence of companion video and photographic evidence, but also because of the abundance of photographic prints from several independent sighting events. The complexity of photographic evidence increased with the surfacing of 110 and 135 format prints in addition to the Polaroid 108 prints. The most exciting factor, however, was the prospect of yet more events to come, since the investigation had begun quite early due to the immediate publication of the first photographs in the local newspaper.

The investigation of any reported sighting of an unidentified flying object has to be subjected to a standard scientific and documented approach, such as that described in the Mutual UFO Network investigator's manual. When such a sighting includes photographic material, it takes on an even more elaborate set of tests and standards. And when a case such as Gulf Breeze comes along, with its unprecedented volume of evidence and numbers of independent witnesses, it requires an enormous effort in investigative documentation, technical analysis and professional cooperation. Nonetheless, I was personally mystified at the premature conclusions that were being drawn from the photographic evidence, well in advance of what was to be an unending mountain of photographic data.

The normal process of case investigations requires the character evaluation of witnesses and photographers, including an examination of their respectability within the community, their financial status and any other factors that might suggest or eliminate their propensity for orchestrating a hoax. It requires an analysis of the circumstances under which the sighting(s) occurred, an examination and testing of photographic equipment, a complete field investigation of the site and a determination of the physical and emotional states of the witness(es).

Due to the ever-increasing work load of the local MUFON investigative team, and in the aftermath of a series of recent photographic analysis discoveries, it was determined by the Fund for UFO Research that they would provide expense funds for me to travel the 1,000-mile trip to Gulf Breeze in order to conduct an in-depth field investigation.

My investigation commenced with a ten-day trip to Gulf Breeze and the surrounding Pensacola area in late December 1988 and early January 1989. At that time I had no idea of what would unfold in the months following the field investigation – the research and subsequent events that occurred in my life would somehow always be connected with my visit to north-west Florida.

This report focuses on a variety of investigative areas of interest directly related to the reports and photographs of UFO activity and the military interest in the events. Two issues prompted me to request a grant from the Fund to pursue a field investigation of my own. One was a report filed by Major George Filer (USAF, retd), following a vacation to the area, which detailed a significant number of unreported witness sightings and apparent abductions. The other was my discovery, through photo analysis, of an apparent abduction event that had yet to be reported, which involved Ed Walters in the presence of his wife Frances.

My field investigations mostly focused on issues raised by sceptics on the case, but culminated in a series of events that left me perplexed and confused as I found myself trying to account for time anomalies and space displacement. During my first visit to Gulf Breeze, I experienced two sighting events, the second resulting in two photographs.

The interviews that I conducted during my investigation included most of the field investigators, witnesses who had previously reported sightings, and numerous other individuals, from bank executives to gas station attendants. Some had seen nothing but were constantly exposed to the night skies, while others had reported their experience only to other respected members of the community. There was a general reluctance to file official reports due to the ever-present publicity surrounding the photographic sighting events which had been published locally and reported on national television programmes. Few of the people I

82

talked to were unaware of the reports of UFOs flying the Gulf Breeze skyline. My impression was that there were at least three times the number of witnesses who had failed to file a report as the 135 that had been publicized at the time.

Ed Walters

Although the character of Ed Walters was a significant issue at the outset, I had developed what I thought was a unique perspective on Ed that dated back to February and March of 1988, when I managed to make contact with him through Duane Cook, editor of the Gulf Breeze *Sentinel*, and succeeded in interviewing him on my radio programme. Eventually, I came to know him well and we became firm friends.

Ed is a successful builder and a highly respected member of his community who has received numerous humanitarian and professional awards. He has made financial contributions (in excess of $100,000) and improvements (including the donation of a theatre) to Gulf Breeze and has demonstrated an interest in the well-being of all the children in his community. If Ed had an ulterior motive in producing his photos and video film, it certainly was not to make money. His annual income far exceeds that of most Americans. Moreover, there is evidence that he sustained considerable losses in business as a result of being publicly acknowledged as the photographer of the pictures published in the local newspaper. This latter declaration no doubt also impacted to a certain extent on his credibility in the community.

In order to develop a professional profile on the veracity of Ed Walters, I arranged for a psychological stress evaluation (PSE) examination of interviews previously conducted with Ed, and interviewed one of the polygraph examiners who had subjected him to a multiple series of polygraph tests. None of the professional examiners could find any evidence of untruthfulness in his extraordinary claims of extraterrestrial visitation, nor could the clinical psychologist Daniel Overlade, PhD., who conducted a battery of psychiatric exams.

Photographic Evaluation

A philosopher once said: 'One picture is worth a thousand words'. In today's high-technology society, where science fiction becomes science fact and fantasy becomes reality, we use higher standards of scrutiny before a stamp of authenticity can be justified. Ed and Frances Walters' photographs have clearly earned such a stamp of approval, in my opinion.

Authentication of the photographic evidence required the expertise of many noted professional analysts, including Dr Bruce Maccabee, and Harry Limbo, the top technical film expert with the Polaroid Corporation in Cambridge, Massachusetts. Dr Maccabee performed the initial analysis using standard acceptable field measurement practices, and evaluated each photograph using optical and/or digital enhancement equipment.

Since the bulk of the photographic evidence was in the form of Polaroid original prints, relatively uncommon in UFO archives, my job became the task of defining the unique chemical process of Polaroid prints and negative peel-off strips, and developing a basis for analysis. The greatest difficulty in the analysis process centred around the facts that the original pictures are extremely dark and the anomalous UFO images are generally quite small. In order to overcome this problem, an independent project was initiated to re-photograph the originals using techniques to increase their overall brightness and to enlarge the subject images for close-up analysis.

My analysis criteria included: evaluation of the effects of expired film dating (involved in the first nine photos); a thorough examination and identification of various film defects; a detailed study of the cameras used, to determine the causes associated with the discovered print emulsion defects and to determine the capability and viability of double exposure techniques which might have been employed, should that be alleged. The study also included an evaluation of how the film type was processed and packaged, and involved a series of experiments that took over seven months to complete. Many of the experiments involved the photographer of the originals, and several took place at the exact site where the original photographs were taken.

In addition to the Polaroid photographic analysis, conducted with the assistance of professional photographer Richard A. Vandenberg, I used my former background credentials as an engineer to gain access to the television production studios at NASA's Goddard Space Flight Center in Greenbelt, Maryland. Electronics engineer Edward Weibe and I conducted a five-month analysis of the video tape taken of a UFO flying over the field behind the Gulf Breeze Senior High School. Omega Studios in Rockville, Maryland, were used to perform an audio analysis of the sound track to the video tape, with the assistance of accoustical physicist John Gardner.

The photographic and video tape analysis in the Gulf Breeze case involved such enormous complexities that we were constantly supported by unreported events simultaneously being investigated. The vastness of the so-called abduction phenomenon that was occurring behind the publicity and controversy in the case demanded as extensive an analysis process as could be sought.

Meterological and site survey analyses were performed as a check against the details reported for the first photographic sighting by Ed Walters. The conclusion verified that the photographs were likely to have been taken on the day and time period reported.

An investigation into the photographic equipment used was conducted through field tests and close consultation with the Polaroid Corporation engineers. It was determined that the camera used up until 7 February 1988 could perform double-exposure techniques with the 108-type film. Investigators provided the primary photographer with a 35 mm Nimslo stereo camera and employed controls that were not subsequently breached, as was determined following inspection of the camera and film after a later photographic sighting.

A more sophisticated Polaroid Sun 600 camera was purchased on 7 March 1988. The camera was first used the following day, during a photographic sighting opportunity. It was determined by the Polaroid engineers that a double exposure was possible, but extremely difficult to effect. On 17 March a second Polaroid Sun 600 was combined with the first in a self-referencing stereo array to create a parallax for measuring the distance and size of the objects by comparing two photographs taken simultaneously. The degree of difficulty for a double-double exposure series was substantially increased beyond a reasonable possibility.

Ed Walters' First Video Film

Another piece of equipment used by Ed Walters was a Sony 8 mm home video camera with sound and without zoom capability. A one minute and thirty-eight second two-part video tape was shot on 28 December 1987.

An extensive analysis of the video film was completed after five months in August 1988. Various enhancement techniques were performed at the Goddard Space Flight Center. Among these tests, a variable-speed element was employed to make tapes for viewing the entire tape at one-tenth speed. A Sony BVU820 video editor model was used with a digital time-base corrector to supply a direct signal to a Tektronix 4632 Video Hard Copy Unit. The thermal printer generated photo images of both phases of each frame. A 10-second portion of the video tape requires 600 single-copy prints. Each print is measured to define altitude, flight path, rotation characteristics, frequency of the 'beacon' light and ring aberrations observed on the craft, as well as attitude in flight, air speed/velocity, acceleration/deceleration, and an analysis of direction reversals.

Analysis of the audio track indicated that no sound could be identified with the object. The analysis was performed by an acoustical physicist who conducted a 'fast orae transform' analysis on the entire audio track. The object observed in the video tape closely resembles objects photographed with the Polaroid cameras. It appears to have a clockwise or left to right rotation. The dome or beacon light blinks on and off at no consistent rate or pattern and displays a variable luminosity with each cycle. The object loses altitude moving to the left of the camera just prior to blinking out.

A ghost image appears in the first phase of the next frame, approximately two object widths to the right, that may be related but is apparently not visible through the transmission medium. There are certain restrictions in the evaluation of the video tape. Due to the horizontal resolution lines, we are viewing the object through what is analogous to jail bars turned sideways. Nonetheless, it appears conclusive that the bottom or power-source light has a variable luminosity characteristic which is not synchronic with the beacon light on top of the object.

The specifications detailed in this case, most notably the absence of audible sound from the UFO in the 8 mm home video and the rotational characteristic, create enormous difficulty when an attempt is made to re-create what is observed by constructing a model to examine the technology. It is quite clear that we are examining a truly anomalous technology.

The following has been learned as a result of the video tape analysis:

1. The craft loses altitude, moving to the left of the camera just prior to blinking out.
2. According to the power-source light emission movements, it appears that the bottom ring is attached closer to the main body of the craft at opposite diameters by a significant margin. The resulting effect is that the ring wobbles even when the craft apparently does not.
3. The craft has a rotation rate of 7.5 cycles per second: one rotation every four frames of the video is conclusively evident.
4. The direction of rotation is consistently clockwise when viewed from below the craft: left to right on a horizontal plane.
5. The dome light blinks on and off at variable rates: 7.5, 10, and 15 cycles per second. (Further research is needed to develop a theory for this discovery.)

The Road Shot

This one photograph (Plate 7.1), taken on 12 January 1988, has received more attention and has been subjected to more scrutiny than perhaps any single UFO photograph. Most amateur analysts have ignored the testimony of the photographer, which is essential to any thorough analysis.

The story itself is as extraordinary as the photograph. Ed Walters was travelling to inspect one of his homes under construction when the 'interception' occurred at about 5.45 p.m. Central Standard Time. (Sceptics misinterpreted white dots in the original Polaroid as rain. Meteorolgical charts proved that there had been no rain for five days before and after that date.) After being forced off the road in his pickup truck, Ed reported that five creatures exited the craft and headed in his direction. He believes that he was then permitted to escape from the scene without a closer encounter, although it is more than possible that an abduction took place. (For further details, see *UFOs: The Gulf Breeze Sightings*, by Ed and Frances Walters, published by Bantam, London, 1990; Morrow, New York, 1990.)

Most analysts of the photograph failed to examine it closely enough to detect an actual build-up of luminescent material under the craft, basing their analysis on the miscalculation that the light was a reflection. That turns out to be a false premise. Upon close examination, it is evident that the photograph depicts a substance that disperses near the crowned surface of the road beneath, close to the double yellow line. There is also evidence of the substance falling out of the craft, as a small wisp of material is clearly visible near the lowest portion of the craft.

Among the many analytical errors made in an effort to discredit the photograph was the argument that the craft's reflection in the hood of the truck was missing. The hood was damaged in a prior accident and rendered a reflection at that angle out of optical impression. The point here is that the complexities involved in thorough photographic analysis go far beyond a casual examination and require access to specific pertinent data. Anything less will result in incorrect conclusions.

Polaroid Photography

Although the uniqueness of Polaroid chemistry presents several advantages over traditional negative film processes, many sceptics have had a field day trying to discredit the Gulf Breeze Polaroid photographs. At issue is the ease with which one can fake photos, particularly with the Polaroid 108-type film, and the effects of improper procedure regarding the processing of the prints.

Sceptics have argued that it is easy to create double exposures with the film. When this is challenged by the evidence, alternative and more complex methods have been alleged, such as the process of cutting out a model and pasting it to a background for a final re-shooting.

The fact of the matter is that creating double exposures is quite easy and requires little in the way of expertise. The problem with many of the UFO photos, however, is that there are obstructions such as trees that darken parts of the UFO image behind them. This is not possible to accomplish with double exposure techniques.

The cut-and-paste method also fails under analysis. A model which was cut out and then pasted on to a background image photograph would have to show sharp edges all around the craft model. The Gulf Breeze photos do not show this at all, since the top and bottom portions of the craft have bright sharp contrasting definition, while the sides tend to blend in with the background image of the sky. This automatically would eliminate either proposed method of hoaxing the photographs.

The use of expired film (exceeding recommended exposure date) and improper processing procedures present additional problems to evaluate. The effects of using expired film are a loss of film speed, a gain in contrast, and a shift toward the blue spectrum for neutral colours. This was, in fact, the case with the first nine photographs taken by Ed Walters, and accounted for the disparity in colour between the photographs and eyewitness testimony.

To begin processing Polaroid 108 film, one must pull the film from the camera and wait for a period of time to allow the chemical processing to take place before peeling off the negative strip. The chemicals are stored in a sealed pouch attached to each print and are activated when the film is pulled through the internal rollers of the camera. Failure to peel the negative strip within approximately 24 hours does not have adverse effects on the processing of the final photographic image. After 24 hours it becomes difficult to remove the negative strip, as the chemicals dry out and act as an adhesive. Further problems might occur at that point, such as cracking and chipping of the print emulsion.

The primary advantage of Polaroid 108-type film is its thick emulsion property. It actually provides a topography which becomes advantageous for analysis purposes, especially if the images are rather dark, such as in night-time photography. Exposing the dark prints to bright light enables one to examine the most minute details latent in the deep emulsion.

Another advantage of the topography feature is that light sources become exceptionally high in contrast when photographed in low light conditions. This allows for detection of precise detail even under the most adverse of conditions and improves the ability to detect double exposure.

It should be noted that the photographs taken by Ed (and Frances) Walters were subjected to the most rigorous scrutiny by several expert professional analysts. No one has been able to prove that even one photograph is the product of photographic trickery.

UFO Model Found

After the UFO photographs were declared authentic, an interesting phenomenon took place in Gulf Breeze. The Pensacola newspaper printed a story in June 1990 about a model that had been found at the former home of Ed Walters. Following the international publicity about the sightings in 1987 and 1988, Ed built a new house and relocated his family. The old residence was on the market for several months and generally accessible to anyone who might wish to enter. It was left unlocked for access by sales agents and the garage door was never locked at any time, even when the house was occupied.

The model was found in the attic above the garage in the spring of 1990 by the new owner, who was tracing the copper water feed tube to the refrigerator ice-maker. It seems that someone had conveniently crimped the copper tube in the attic, just by the place where Ed supposedly had stashed his UFO model neatly under some loose attic insulation.

The model itself was strikingly similar to a drawing made by Ed Walters in 1988 and published in the local Gulf Breeze *Sentinel*. Upon close examination it was learned that the model was made from styrofoam plates and construction paper, much like that used by Ed in his preliminary designs for custom-built homes. Upon further examination it was proven to be from a discarded design, and actually verified by notarized statement of the clients to have been drawn in September 1989, well after all of the photographs had been taken and published. Furthermore, the model did not resemble the actual photos but did resemble a published drawing.

The sceptics would have us believe that Ed Walters, who was clever enough to hoax photographs that could not be detected by experts, was foolish enough to leave behind a model of which there was no photographic likeness. He then further implicated himself by crimping the water line to the ice-maker by accident. I find it difficult to accept that a professional custom builder would be so careless in this regard.

Photographic Controversy

UFO photographic analysts hear stories of hoaxed pictures on a regular basis. It is rare, however, for an analyst to be confronted with a genuine hoax. The case of Tommy Smith Jr, of Gulf Breeze, fits into an as yet unregistered class in photographic analysis. According to my investigation and analysis, I don't believe there has ever been a case reported where a UFO photographer has turned in pictures that he reportedly hoaxed, yet the analysis clearly suggests that they are authentic.

Tommy, who presented the photographs, initially reported that they were created as double exposures, using a model as the UFO and naming Ed Walters as the photographer. Rounding out the dichotomy, Ed naturally refutes this testimony through a qualified polygrapher.

The negatives were submitted as a set of twelve 110 format exposures. Upon examination, it was evident that the negatives relating to the UFO photos did not originate from the same strip of film as the other six negatives. The other six photos do, however, represent an apparent connection to the Smith family, and there was no immediate clarification regarding the attempt to connect them to the UFO negatives.

The results of all this confusion have distracted us from the ultimate task of determining the more imperative issue regarding the authenticity of the UFO images. If they are genuine images of a craft, then the entire scenario regarding the actual photographer takes on a more dynamic episode of sociological manipulation, regardless of who took the pictures. There exists yet another interesting social dichotomy in the event that the photos prove to be fabricated, which would make the determination of the actual photographer even more critical.

The analysis process required access to the original negatives. Using these, we were able to generate a series of prints developed at various exposure levels in order to get a broader view of the activity taking place at the time the photos were taken. Overexposed prints revealed the smallest details of the object in the pictures as well as the surrounding foreground and background. Underexposed prints enabled us to get a closer detailed look at the light source(s) which generated the images on to the negative strips when the shutter was triggered.

Once this process was completed, we moved on to the next step in the analysis procedure, which involved identifying the components on each print and conducting a series of measurements to approximate size comparisons. Since the camera that was used to take the pictures was not available, we could still make some general predictions based on the standard focal length of 110 format cameras. The UFO images appearing in those photographs were compared to other similar photos taken by various photographers in the same region over the past couple of years. All of this data was then assembled and assimilated with other known data to determine what conclusions could be drawn.

The following is what has been learned from the analysis of the photographic negatives presented by Tommy Smith:

1. The images are the product of single exposures as opposed to double exposures, since there exists no background or second overlay image.
2. The images are of extraordinarily high contrast for 110 mm format, indicating a high luminosity light source at the bottom of this primary object.
3. The series of images depict the typical rocking motion of the craft, as seen in other photographic series and reported by witnesses in other events in the same area.
4. The craft represents an exact generic match to other photographs of this type of craft taken in the same area and reported by hundred of witnesses.
5. The object appears to contain a self-generated light source of extreme intensity and does not cast skyglow effects on the obstructions between the camera and the lighted object.
6. The object appears in a slightly different position and attitude in each of the succeeding exposures relative to the camera and the obstruction, suggesting a low probability of a staged environment studio creation using a model.
7. The object appears to be at a distance of 30–50 feet from the camera, with an obstruction most probably at a distance of 2–6 feet in front of the camera. The object measures approximately 14–20 feet in diameter. Shape: 3-dimensional, cylindrical.
8. There exists a self-luminescent beacon post on top of the object which extends at differing lengths out of the object in the series of exposures. This is a unique finding that corroborates previously reported testimony in other cases in the same geographical area. The luminosity level of this feature varies with each photographic image in the series and differs significantly from the primary light source at the bottom of the object, again creating an extremely low probability of a model construction as opposed to a complex aeroform with self-propelled airborn hovering characteristics.
9. The lower ring, or shroud, around the bottom of the craft appears to exhibit a dynamic pulsing motion as it measures at different distances from the main body in the series of images. This suggests

a complex construction analogous to a series of photographs of an airplane in flight which depict the movement in its wing flaps or rudder components – although clearly these are not images of any known aircraft. This feature further diminishes the possibility of a simple model as an explanation for the object photographed.

10. The negatives reveal a series of lights around the main body of the object that matches generically with other photographs taken in the area, and presents a continuing expression of complex automated electronics or similar technology.

In conclusion, the photographic negatives presented by Tommy Smith Jr represent, in my opinion, a series of images of a genuine UFO encounter photographed at a circular cul-de-sac in Gulf Breeze, Florida, as the photographer stepped behind a palm tree offering some degree of protection against a possible perceived threat from the object. The object photographed is airborn, self-propelled, probably intelligently piloted, and hovering at an altitude most probably not exceeding 50 feet above ground level.

Research into similar events would suggest that the photographer probably has little knowledge of other events that occurred during this close-up photographic sighting. In other words, due to the close proximity of the object, it is unlikely that the photographer got away without being intercepted by the intelligence operating the unidentified craft.

Historical research has indicated that in typical events of this nature, memory can be and usually is suppressed beyond the recollection capability of the individual. Clinical hypnosis has been effective in recapturing partial or total recall of such encounter events.

Interviews with friends of the photographer revealed that the photographer was indeed Tommy Smith Jr, and the scene at which the pictures were taken coincides with the obstructions observed in the actual photographs. Further testimony suggested that the photographs were probably taken a few days before Ed Walters had taken his first Polaroid pictures in November 1987.

The photographs and video film taken by Ed Walters and others in Gulf Breeze represent genuine physical objects of unknown origin. The analyses have determined approximate size and distance relationships with the surrounding terrain. The variety of equipment used to photograph the objects leaves a very narrow window of low probability for an exotic deception. My year-long character evaluation of the primary photographer, Ed Walters, removes all doubt, for me, relating to his ability to perpetrate any such deception. The evidence, in my estimation, will support itself through time.

Government Interest

On 9 May 1988, I initiated an official appeal for assistance through the Office of the President of the United States and various members of the Senate and House of Representatives. Government or at least military interest in the events which were occurring in Gulf Breeze was apparent in the light of newspaper reports bearing photographs of vessels with elaborate radar gear; military vehicles with telescoping radar gear (all deployed in the vicinity of the sightings); and a reported visit to Ed Walters' residence by purported officials requesting original photographic materials.

Responses received by me from the Office of the Secretary of the Navy revealed concern over evidence of federal airspace rules violations, and responses from congressional representation revealed concern over human rights violations. The Office of the Chief of Naval Operations (Air Warfare) ultimately declined to investigate, citing scarce Navy financial and personnel resources.

Just a few months later, in August 1988, the Joint Chiefs of Staff met at the Pensacola Naval Air Station under strict security. The following month, after I filed an official complaint with the US Postal Service, an almost year-long bout of tampering with Ed Walters' mail mysteriously stopped.

Personal Experiences

In December 1988 I was alone on a late-night research effort at the Players Golf and Country Club resort, where Duane Cook had video-filmed Ed Walters photographing a UFO on 24 January that year. I was investigating the prospects of a sighting feasibility by two of Duane's associates from the *Sentinel*, who had followed in a car not far behind Ed's truck, but unbeknownst to Ed and Duane.

I had been keeping tight records with regular time checks when, less than ten minutes after a time check recording, it suddenly became quite warm in the car. This could easily have been a result of my rather efficient auto heater. The temperature outside the car was typically chilly for December in north-west Florida – not exactly beach weather. I rolled down the electric window on the driver's door and leaned my head back to rest on the support that divides the front and back doors, looking up into the night sky.

Immediately, I noticed something odd about the three stars that form the belt in the constellation of Orion. Instead of the familiar three stars equidistant in a row, there were clearly five such stars. I pondered this for what seemed no less than two minutes when I realized that I was suddenly quite chilly. Pushing the button to roll up the window, I glanced at the digital clock just above the glove box on the passenger side of the car. To my utter amazement, it appeared as though at least 15–20 minutes had passed by instead of the two or three that I felt had elapsed. I quickly checked my notepad to confirm the last time check and looked again at the clock, only to realize that it had in fact been more than an hour and twenty minutes since my last time check.

As I checked my wristwatch to verify the time on the car clock, I glanced up through the front window and discovered that I was no longer at the Players Club but in fact had mysteriously relocated to Soundside Drive, and was parked in the same location where Ed Walters had manoeuvred his truck during an incident on 12 January 1988. I have never been able to rationalize this strange event.

During the course of my field investigations, I also experienced two unusual sightings in the Gulf Breeze area. The first took place in late December 1988 while travelling with Ed Walters in his truck across the Three Mile Bridge to Pensacola. Local MUFON chief Charles Flannigan was following in his vehicle behind us while the sighting took place just left of our position crossing the bridge.

The object was little more than 200 feet out over the water at an altitude of approximately 50 feet above sea level, moving at comparable velocity with us, parallel at first then drifting away at the same speed. As the object moved away, it was possible to see a reflection on the water of the golden-orange ring on the bottom of the craft. The sighting lasted approximately 2–3 minutes as the object disappeared from view near the pier area on the Pensacola shoreline.

I had a fully automatic camera resting on my lap during the entire event as Ed and I tried to determine what the object was, but it never occurred to either of us to take a picture. Charles was unaware of the event that was taking place and it did not occur to us to attempt to signal to him at the time.

Just a couple of days later, late in the evening of 2 January 1989, I had decided to make one last visit to Shoreline Park after I had packed for my return drive back to Maryland. It was approximately 1.00 a.m. when I decided to rest and take in the ambience of the setting at the picnic table made famous by several of Ed Walters' UFO photographs. The night was still and I could feel the tranquil silence of the Santa Rosa Sound as I peered out across the horizon at Pensacola Beach. The sky had a blackness to it that blocked out the stars with haze.

As my eyes followed the opposite shoreline of houses, hotels and streetlights dotting the way to Fort Pickens State Park, I noticed an odd light that was too high to be a boat but too close to the water to be any kind of land vehicle. The lack of sound eliminated the possibility of a helicopter. The object was moving along the shoreline, occasionally retracing its flight path before continuing toward the Bob Sykes Bridge. I quickly grabbed my camera which was mounted on a mini-tripod on the picnic table and snapped two pictures at the fully zoomed setting.

The object moved more quickly to my left and became obstructed by a bush beside the picnic table. For a moment I panicked when the object appeared to move closer toward me, but in fact it had only increased its altitude as it moved up over the toll booth at the base of the bridge to clear the water tanks along the shoreline. In order to get a better view, I left my position behind the picnic table and ran toward the parking lot, glancing up to see if there was anyone else with whom I could share this observation.

When my eyes quickly returned to scanning the horizon near the toll booth to relocate the object, panic once again set in as I was unable to locate the object in the night sky amidst the backdrop of lights on the opposite shoreline. I recall feeling extremely vulnerable at that point as I scanned up and around in every direction, not knowing where the object might pop up at any moment.

Seeking cover under the thatched roof of a picnic table on the beach, the silence of the night was broken by the roar of turbines coming from distinctively military jets approaching from the right in the vicinity of Pensacola Naval Air Station. They ripped through the night sky just in front of me out over the Santa Rosa Sound, disappearing in the direction I last saw the strange lighted object. I thought it odd that they displayed no lights of any kind – not even standard navigation lights – as they scrambled through the canopy of a cloud layer that was fully illuminated by the sky-glow created by ground lights.

My excitement was only exceeded by the nervousness that I felt upon realizing how foolish it was to be out there all alone in the night. Sometimes our eagerness to learn about the mysteries of the universe takes us to the very frontiers of reality, and we forget about the prospects of terror that have consumed some of those who have gone before us. Perhaps it is this neglect for the fear of the unknown that will enable us to cross the threshold which binds us to our unknown origins and the limits of our present consciousness.

The two photographs turned out to be an exact match of the last object which Ed Walters had photographed on 1 May 1988, as he inadvertently triggered the right hand camera in the Self-Referencing Stereo array (SRS – designed by Dr Bruce Maccabee) just before being neurologically paralyzed by the intelligence aboard the craft that had moved in overhead.

On 4 July 1990, my wife and I had enjoyed a pleasant evening taking in the fireworks display on Pensacola Beach. We had come to Florida on vacation for a few days, prior to the MUFON Symposium to be held that weekend in Pensacola. Our view from the eighth floor of the Pensacola Beach Holiday Inn offered a wide panoramic scene of the Gulf of Mexico, and the Gulf breeze and cadence of the surf beckoned us to leave the balcony door open throughout the night.

I awoke abruptly at 4.00 a.m. and bolted right out of bed. It was never resolved just what it was that woke me, but whatever the reason (if only to use the toilet) it was certainly not a normal habit. The first thing I did once out of bed was to peer out of the balcony as a bright light on the horizon caught my eye. It was curious that it did not seem to be moving at all, not even the slight yaw and pitch of a ship afloat on the sea. It was extremely brilliant and lit up the horizon in the darkness, to the point where it became easy to see the separation of sky and sea. There were occasional aircraft visible, but not in the vicinity of whatever this was, and they paled considerably in size and brilliance by comparison.

Mary was awakened by the commotion as I fumbled for my video camera. She too was awed by the sight that I was now filming. After several minutes, the object failed to move as I calibrated its position against the vertical supports of the balcony railing. Mary went back to bed as I mounted my 35 mm Pentax on to the tripod to get some still photos.

Thirty minutes into this sighting, with most of a 36-exposure roll of film used, a second object appeared on the horizon as the first began to change into a slow rhythmic pulsing light. Awake for the second time, Mary arrived on the balcony in time to see the two objects merge into one as I captured the event on film. Only seconds later, the merged object changed colour from a brilliant white to a brilliant green. At the time of the merging, the entire horizon was lit up as if it were daylight.

At about 5.00 a.m., everything disappeared into darkness as the first signs of dawn began to appear in the east. I was unable to go back to bed, consumed with excitement. I had the film developed that morning. The results were successful, and I had captured the incredible merging of the two objects, frame by frame.

When the MUFON investigators learned about this photographic sighting there was a slight sense of resentment, since they spend much of their time attempting to witness just such an event. Within hours of my arrival in the area, here I was for the third time in the middle of such bizarre activity. Upon seeing the photographic evidence, however, the investigators remarked that it was the best case they had had there in months.

In the years to come, 5 July will be for me as commemorative as 4 July!

The Phenomena Continue

If the Gulf Breeze UFO case was based only on the Ed Walters photographs, then one might expect that the novelty would be well worn off by now. The fact of the matter is that it is not just an Ed Walters case. As we wrap up the fourth year since the first published UFO photographs surfaced, it is time to reflect on what actually has happened in Gulf Breeze, Florida.

Over 250 reported sightings of UFOs, other than those by Ed Walters, are documented. Over 500 witnesses have actually been named in those sighting reports. The sightings have never completely stopped but in fact have come in waves or cycles. There exist numerous video films, some taken by professional film crews from network television companies. Over 100 photographs have been taken by numerous photographers, using all formats of film, including infra-red. One of the video films taken in May 1988 did not surface until November 1990, and shows ten objects over the water.

We have seen documented and recorded evidence of the following: telepathic communication, analyzed by a professional psychologist; biological material recovered from an abduction encounter which was determined to be from a silica-based organism unknown to science; unusual liquid apparently jettisoned from a UFO was recovered which apparently bubbled without giving off heat for several weeks. In addition, clinical psychologists have worked with dozens of victims of UFO abduction experiences – encounters that have shown unique correlations among unrelated victims.

One of the most extraordinary incidents occurred in November 1989. An unexplained phenomenon called a skyquake was reported over the region, followed shortly thereafter by the discovery of an area of swirled grass, much like the Circle phenomenon in the UK and elsewhere. Two months later, the same two events occurred again. Most curious of all, the measurements of the Circles precisely coincided with the known derived measurements of the base of most of the UFOs photographed by Ed Walters (14–15 feet). These were quite unlike the famous Circle found behind the Gulf Breeze High School in December 1987. In that case, the grass appeared to have been subjected to excessive amounts of energy that removed the chlorophyl from the grass, which died immediately. No evidence of radioactivity was discovered in any of these cases.

It can be reported that I have never yet been to this attractive city and not been fortunate to bear witness to some extraordinary events. In January 1991 I brought an ABC TV crew to Gulf Breeze and successfully obtained a recorded sighting for national broadcast. And in May 1991 I brought a film crew from Nippon Television Network to Gulf Breeze to shoot a Japanese documentary, and again was successful in obtaining a video-recorded sighting.

Whatever is mysteriously flying in the skies over north-west Florida is still there and is available for anyone to experience. Regardless of one's conclusions about Gulf Breeze, it seems evident that an unknown or at least unidentified intelligence has initiated the equivalent of a *glasnost* policy of its own there. We can only speculate what the year 1992 will bring to Gulf Breeze.

8

Puerto Rico's Astounding UFO Situation

JORGE MARTÍN

Leading Puerto Rican investigator Jorge Martín is the editor of *Enigma!*, a monthly magazine featuring articles on UFOs and the paranormal. He has investigated hundreds of UFO incidents in the island of Puerto Rico since 1975, and has written many articles and reports for Puerto Rican newspapers as well as many foreign magazines.

Jorge Martín's article published in *The UFO Report 1991* dealt with his investigations into two incidents in 1988 when US Navy jet fighters were apparently abducted by UFOs in the Cabo Rojo area, observed by over 100 witnesses. In August 1990 I visited Puerto Rico in order to meet some of the principal witnesses, and came away with the conviction that these extraordinary incidents had in fact taken place as described.

We present here a follow-up on some of the many incidents that have occurred subsequently in this US territorial possession in the Caribbean; important incidents with profound implications, as we shall see.

In *The UFO Report 1991* I informed readers about a shocking incident that happened on 28 December 1988, when two US Navy jet fighters were 'abducted' in mid-air by a huge triangle-shaped UFO in the Cabo Rojo area, and another similar incident which occurred on 16 November that year, in the Guama area of San Germán, a town about 20 miles from Cabo Rojo. Many more incidents such as these have happened since 31 May 1987, when the UFO 'flap' began in our country.

UFO Chase in El Yunque

On 4 July 1989, several witnesses who live in the Sabana/Yuquiyú sector of the town of Luquillo – an area next to the National Caribbean Rain Forest – were able to see a UFO, described as a 'bright starlike oval object', being chased by two jet fighters that had been scrambled from the

Figure 8:1. Location of El Yunque incident.
Roosevelt Roads Naval Station is at lower right.

nearby Roosevelt Roads Naval Station in Ceiba. (Figure 8.1)

According to Rosa Dávila de Quiñones, a resident in the Sabana sector (the only witness willing to be identified), there was an electrical power blackout in the area that night. At about 8.30 p.m., as she discussed this with her neighbours, they all saw the UFO flying over the rain forest and the El Yunque mountain, where many such incidents have been reported.

'At first it looked like a very big and brilliant blue-white star,' said Mrs Dávila, 'but then it began moving fast and doing several high-speed angled turns, and that's when we all realized it was something strange – something not normal.'

She explained that after several passes and turns over the mountains in the rain forest, the UFO began descending, heading directly at a 45-degree angle toward the El Yunque mountain. Then they all saw two jet fighters approaching the area from the east, heading towards the UFO. All the witnesses were sure that the fighters had been sent from Roosevelt Roads Naval Station, and watched as they began closing in on the luminous object. At that moment, the UFO changed course at high speed and lit up more brightly with a white light, disappearing in the sky over the Pitahaya Mountains, to the south-east of the Luquillo Mountain range, still pursued by the jets. All the neighbours were astonished by this sight.

Coincidentally, I was in the El Yunque area that same day, checking on other UFO reports, and I can therefore confirm that there was a power failure in Rio Grande and Luquillo. Unfortunately, I left at 7.30 p.m., thus missing the UFO/jets incident, which I could have filmed with my video camera.

'Ball of Light' in Guavate

On Friday 22 June 1990 José Antonio Valdés, his wife Matilde and a military friend of theirs who was visiting them at their home, were all witnesses to another startling UFO encounter.

At 6.30 p.m., the two men were making some repairs at Valdés wooden house in the Los Piñero sector in Guavate, Cayey, in the eastern central part of the island (see Figure 8:2), when all of a sudden they saw a large, strange 'ball of light' fly over Valdés' house at great speed. The UFO was described as 'a round ball of bright yellow light with a very bright red light in its centre'. No more details could be observed. According to the witnesses, the ball of light was flying horizontally 'on a north-east to south-west trajectory', and as soon as it had passed over them, 'four military jets appeared as if trailing or chasing it at high speed'.

The jets were described as of a 'blueish-grey metallic colour, with two "booster" engines, and all of them had their wings positioned backwards and flew very fast' (see Figure 8:3).

This description fits with that of US Navy F-14 Tomcat jets. 'The jets were flying very low over the area and circling the sky,' according to the witnesses, 'as if searching for something, then they left in the same direction the ball of light took – to the south-west – and disappeared.' The apparent size of the UFO was estimated at three times the size of the jets they all saw. Therefore, the object must have been about 180 feet in diameter.

Figure 8:2. The arrow indicates the spot where José Antonio Valdés, his wife Matilde and their military friend saw the UFO being chased by two F-14s and an AWACS plane. The star pinpoints the encounter site.

Figure 8:3 (right). Sketch by Antonio Valdés.
Figure 8:4. The 'ball of light' as drawn by Matilde Valdés.

'Only 5 or 6 minutes had elapsed after the jets flew over the area when we all saw a big jet with a round flattened thing on top fly over, in the same direction the UFO and fighters had previously taken,' said Valdés. According to a military officer we interviewed there, that last big jet was

was an AWACS (Airborne Early Warning and Control System) plane, and he and the other witnesses were sure that the UFO was being chased by both the fighters and the AWACS plane, all of them coming from the direction of the Roosevelt Roads Naval Station.

The officer stated his certainty that what he saw was a pursuit and search operation by the AWACS plane and fighters. 'I come frequently to this area, and this is not the first time I've seen UFOs here,' he said. 'On many occasions you can see these objects flying around, and then suddenly they descend into certain mountain areas and disappear there. To me, these military aircraft – especially the AWACS plane – were trying to locate the place these objects possibly go to. Maybe they go underground somewhere, and that's what they're checking.'

The UFO they all observed was totally soundless and very bright. Similar UFOs have frequently been seen in the Guavate region, and I have investigated a number of the sightings. We have the officer's name and address, but he asked us not to disclose his name or rank for fear of possible harassment. We have several witnesses to our interview with him who are prepared to come forward and verify what he said, should there be any need to do so.

'Playful' UFO

On 28 June 1990 José Rodríguez, a resident in the Barrio Playita area of Yabucoa (see map) to the east of the island, near the Roosevelt Roads Naval Station, saw another surprising chase of a UFO by US military planes. 'The UFO played with the jets, outdodging them at great speed for a couple of minutes, then flew off very fast and disappeared to the south-west, still followed by the jets from a distance,' he told us.

An Encounter at an Army Reserve Base

The following account was given to us by a confidential source, a military officer stationed at the US Army Reserve Base at Fort Allen, in Juana Díaz, southern Puerto Rico. After we agreed not to disclose his name or rank, he explained what happened on the night of 18–19 July 1990 at 12.10 a.m.

According to the officer, the soldiers and officers at the base that night were all in the barracks, except for those on duty, when suddenly the base perimeter was lit up with a powerful white light. Our source explained that at that very moment a high-ranking officer gave the order over the base intercom for 'everyone to stay indoors and not to come out of the barracks or any other base facilities under any circumstances'.

The light was very bright, but when the order was given he was already looking out through a window. What he saw gave him a shock.

'In an area towards the coast, just over the base and a little to the south, there was a brightly lit disc-like object. It was circular and metallic-looking, as if it was made of aluminium. It had what seemed like many windows on its centre edge, with yellowish-white lights revolving in them. At the underside of the object there was a round turbine-like protrusion with many coloured lights around it [see the sketch by the officer, Figure 8.5], and from underneath the object came a very bright beam of pinkish-white light, as if searching for something. That same light was the one illuminating the base perimeter.'

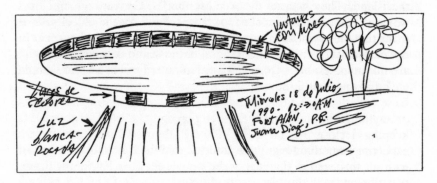

Figure 8:5.

The officer stood there for a moment, transfixed, not believing his own eyes. All of a sudden, he said,

'I heard the loud sound of jet engines, and two jets flew at high speed over the base. To me, the jets were of the F-18 Hornet type, and were scrambled from somewhere to check on the UFO next to the base. As soon as the jets headed in the direction of the UFO, the object departed at speed to the west with the sound of rushing wind, followed by the jets. Those planes must have been scrambled from the Roosevelt Roads Naval Station, because to the best of my knowledge there are no F-18s in the Muñiz National Guard Air Base in Isla Verde. They must have come from an aircraft carrier participating in the UNITAS manoeuvres at Roosevelt Roads and on Vieques Island, because normally there are no F-18s based in Puerto Rico.'

What the officer said next came as a surprise.

'Something big is happening here with all this UFO activity. Recently, all the military personnel in Fort Allen were shown several video films which informed us about the reality of UFOs. They showed us an old black-and-white film about a UFO crash that supposedly happened in New Mexico many years ago. We all saw the craft, which was semi-buried in the ground at a 45-degree angle, and there were several bodies of the crew. According to what we were shown, these bodies were about five feet tall, thin, very pale, and had large bald heads. They had big round eyes and a small nose, but I don't recall any mouths or ears.'

'They also showed us another video of UFOs filmed by them around the island. They wanted us to know that UFOs are real, but they wouldn't elaborate when asked for more details. You know, it seemed to me that they wanted us to know this was real and that the beings were not perfect: they are fallible, their crafts crash and they also die – they are not invulnerable. Apparently, they wanted to condition us to the idea that they exist, and to accept the possibility of someday having to liaise with them. The officers wouldn't say that these were alien crafts or anything like, just that they were real and that the Government is keeping a close eye on them. Finally, they told us that they are expecting something big: they wouldn't explain what, but it had to do with all this, and if that happened we would have to deal with the situation and with the people – the public.'

This report, given to us by our confidential source in Fort Allen, was later confirmed by two other independent military sources who approached us at the UFO Photo Stand which we shared with John Timmerman of the J. Allen Hynek Center for UFO Studies (CUFOS), in Plaza Las Américas Shopping Mall, San Juan, during the week of 13–18 August 1990. Apparently, special military groups on the island have been receiving official briefings on the UFO situation since 1988, the year in which the jet fighters were abducted by the huge triangular-shaped UFOs in Cabo Rojo and San Germán.

Let us now turn to some further important developments in other parts of the island.

Five Humanoid Creatures in the Road

At the beginning of September 1990, following the visit of Timothy Good, who had come to the island to interview the principal witnesses to the 1988 sightings, another investigator, the journalist Bob Pratt (co-author with Philip Imbrogno and Dr J. Allen Hynek of *Night Siege: The Hudson Valley UFO Sightings*, Ballantine, New York 1987), visited Puerto Rico to check these incidents. While investigating in the Laguna Cartagena area, we contacted Benito Collado, an employee of the Caribe gas station at the entrance of road 101 from Lajas to the tourist resort Boquerón, Cabo Rojo.

Collado discussed the seriousness of the UFO situation, adding that he himself had seen on several occasions 'big red balls of light that make strange movements in the sky very quickly, then descend very slowly into the Laguna Cartagena in a vertical fashion, as if in a controlled manner'. 'Something big is happening here,' he added. 'Last week, the owner of the cafe El Tamarindo had an experience with some large-headed little men – some weird creatures there in the road.'

Already knowing about the incident, thanks to our friend José Pérez, who had spoken to Collado, we (Bob Pratt and I, together with Wilson Sosa, our collaborator from Cabo Rojo who had been a witness to one of the 1988 incidents) visited Miguel Figueroa, the witness, at his small cafeteria. Figueroa, a chubby 55-year-old man, was reluctant at first to describe his incredible experience, but eventually agreed to tell us.

'You know,' he began, 'you don't talk about these things because people say you are crazy. And I don't blame them, because they haven't seen anything. I was like that. I used to deny these things, but now that it's happened to me, I know that it's all real . . .'

We told him that we were seriously interested in what had happened, and Mr Figueroa, still nervous and bewildered, began to explain.

'It was in the early hours of Friday 31 August 1990, at about 3.30 a.m. I was at home and had a dream that someone had got into my cafe, and I woke up, worried. So I got dressed, got into my car and went to the cafe to check if everything was all right. When I arrived, there were about ten cars parked there in the front, and several people who seemed to be alarmed about something. Thinking that maybe something had happened at my cafe, I continued on, made a turn, looked around, then came back and asked some of the people what was going on.

'A woman, very alarmed, was screaming about "The little men, the little men!" Some other guys there, also very nervous, explained that they were all driving down road 101 in their cars when all of a sudden a bunch of strange little big-headed men or "Martians" appeared, walking in the same road. They all stopped their cars at my cafe's parking lot, refusing to move. In the meantime, the woman continued screaming hysterically. "That's nonsense!", I said. "There are no little men". And I laughed at them. Anyway, when they insisted, I started my car and went down the road just to have a look for myself.

'Almost a kilometre away, I saw them. My God, I thought, what is this? There, some 50 feet away in the road in front of me were five incredible things! Lord, why did this have to happen to me? I was very frightened by what I saw, but at the same time I felt fascinated. I wanted to see more, so I began following them from a distance. It was incredible. I remember it all and still get very nervous. Since that night I haven't been able to sleep; I'm always thinking about them.

'They were five of the strangest creatures I have ever seen. The biggest one was about 5 feet tall, and the smallest one about 3 feet tall. They were skinny, with large pear-shaped heads, long pointy ears, big slanted eyes and almost no nose – only small holes. Their mouths were almost like a slit – very little. They all had long arms with three fingers on each hand and three toes on their feet. At their elbows and knees they had something that looked like joints, but I don't know – I'm not sure about that. I don't know if that was part of some clothing they had on, but to me they seemed to be naked. They were greyish, from head to toes: at least, that is what it seemed to me' (see drawing based on Figueroa's description, Figure 8:6).

Figure 8:6.

'I was scared to death, but I had to see them more closely so I kept following them in my car, and at a certain point I got really close to

107

them. That's when the taller one turned around and looked at me with those big bright eyes. Then the others turned around, and at that moment a very bright light, like welding light, came out of their eyes and blinded me for a moment. My car's lights were on, but the light coming out from their eyes was much, much brighter. I was blinded and scared, then I stopped the car and heard – I don't know if that's the correct way of describing it – I felt, or heard something telling me not to get any closer.

'When I regained my sight, they were walking down the road again, and I began following them once more, this time from an increased distance. When they arrived at the bridge they jumped over it one by one and went down by the small creek that runs below the bridge to the south, and disappeared walking into it until I couldn't see them any more.'

We asked Figueroa if he knew where that small river led to. 'To the Laguna Cartagena,' he replied reluctantly. He had been unable to believe what he had seen. 'I knew it was real, that I was seeing them, but it was incredible. I thought I was going crazy. When they disappeared in the river, I went back and told the people what I saw, then went home. I tried to sleep, but couldn't. I kept seeing their images – those faces, those eyes . . .

Figueroa continued with his account, sweating and obviously deeply affected by the experience. 'The next morning, I went back to the place, and the little men's three-toed footprints were still there in the river mud. I went back later at noon, and they were still there. I was not crazy! It did happen, the tracks are still there! Too bad I didn't think of getting a camera and photographing the tracks, because the next day it rained heavily and they disappeared.

'This has ruined my life. I'm not the same man since that night. Why did it have to be me?,' he kept saying. At first, Figueroa would not tell us why he was reluctant to discuss his encounter with the beings, but later on, when he trusted us more, explained that he had been threatened. 'By whom?' we asked. He looked worried.

'I don't know. Late the next day I received a phone call, and a man speaking in Spanish with an American accent told me not to talk or say anything to anyone about what I had seen and where the little men had gone into [the Laguna Cartagena, scene of most UFO incidents in the area], and that if I did, something bad could happen to me. That was it! I was already scared by what I had seen, and then that . . . What worried me most is how he obtained my telephone number, because it is on a private line, and what's more, it is listed under another person's name. Even so, the man who called wanted to talk directly to me, Miguel Figueroa. How could he have known? I still can't explain it.'

Miguel is convinced that what he saw on the early hours of 31 August 1990 is related to the many UFO incidents reported in this area.

'At first I wouldn't tell you, but I have seen UFOs, or flying saucers, in this area before. And I'm telling you, what is happening here is real, and these beings must have a base or something underground in this area. I don't think they are aggressive. I was alone, and that light they emitted indicated that they are powerful; even so, they didn't harm me. They could have, but they didn't. It was as if they were telling me not to get any closer . . . I only wish this hadn't occurred, because I can't deal with it – I would like to forget it all.'

Even though many people saw the other witnesses outside the cafe that night, no one knows their names or addresses, and Miguel Figueroa is the only one to come forward so far.

[Editor's note: By an interesting coincidence, I was in the Laguna Cartagena area on the afternoon of 31 August 1990, about 12 hours after the alleged encounter, together with Jorge Martín, Wilson Sosa, my girlfriend and another investigator. Needless to say, we saw nothing.]

A Strange Craft at Oliveras

While we were talking to Figueroa, another man, Luis Diodonet, told us about a strange craft he had seen on the night of 17 August 1990, next to the aerostat [balloon] facility of Oliveras. After being introduced to us by Benito Collado, Diodonet guided us to the exact spot where he saw the craft, just in front of the dumping site next to the aerostat installation, and described the sighting:

'I was driving on this road in the Oliveras area at about 2.00 a.m., after leaving some friends in Las Palmas to go home when suddenly I got here and saw a very weird thing there in front of the mountain, and stopped my car and got out to have a better look. It was some-thing strange, suspended in mid-air over that mountain that divides this sector from La Parguera sector, just in the farm administered by Freddie Guindin. Look, it was rather like one of those so-called flying

109

saucers, but it had something on top. You know the conical upper part of witches' hats! It was like that, conical on top and a circular base around it. (See Plate 8.5.)

'It was big and had many lights around it, and it looked silvery-metallic. But the strangest thing was that something was coming out from underneath it, like a swirling mist that went directly down to the mountain in a column, but swirling in a spiralling column. That column was semi-luminous; a column of light and clouds or mist coming down from that object . . . I do believe that thing was an OVNI [UFO].'

'I said to myself, What a strange thing! I had never seen anything like that. And you could hear a humming sound coming from it. It just stood there, and after looking at it for a while, I left . . . The policemen who patrol that place [the aerostat facility] surely saw it too, because it was on top of the mountain at the entrance to the place, so there's no doubt in my mind that they must have seen it. If I heard the humming sound coming from it here, they must have heard it louder there, because they were nearer to it.

'I don't know, but we have a feeling here that the aerostat has nothing to do with the drugs problem, as the Government wants us to believe. We think it has something to do with the UFOs that are being seen here, maybe to keep an eye on them.'

Luis made it clear that at first he was reluctant to discuss what he had seen, fearing no one would believe him, but after hearing us talk to Miguel Figueroa he realized the importance of what he saw in relation to the UFO situation in the area, and changed his mind, for which we thank him deeply.

Interesting though it was, there was nothing to back up Luis' story. However, while visiting the home of Roosevelt Acosta (another UFO witness), his sister Dolin and her daughters and a son-in-law all stated that in the early hours of 17 August, while going to Roosevelt's home, they all saw a strange craft over a mountain next to the aerostat. It was at about 2–2.30 a.m. when they saw what looked like 'a flying saucer with a pointed thing on top, with many lights. It came flying from the west and suspended itself over that mountain [the same one identified by Diodonet], and something like smoke came down from it in a swirling motion to the ground.'

The sighting was corroborated! Four totally independent witnesses saw the same object reported by Diodonet at the same time and in the same place. Dolin Acosta and her family said they observed the UFO for about an hour, after which they went to sleep, not knowing what happened to it after that.

UFO Chased by Helicopters

At 5.30 p.m. on 19 December 1990, Mario Orlando Rodríguez, a resident of the Bairoa Park urban development in Caguas in the central eastern part of Puerto Rico, saw a sight that he will never forget. According to his report, Rodríguez, who is a freelance commercial graphic artist, was working in his studio at home that afternoon when he heard the sound of helicopters flying very low over his house. His curiosity aroused, he went outside to see what was going on and, to his surprise and amazement, witnessed something he never expected to see.

'When I came out I saw dark green military helicopters with no markings, numbers or identification, flying very low over the houses. They seemed like the ordinary choppers used by the P.R. National Air Guard. One of them had an opening on its side and there was a man clinging out, tied or strapped with some type of belt. The man was shouting something I couldn't hear because of the helicopters' engines, and he was pointing in a specific direction. When I looked in that direction, there was a weird thing there . . . It was like a big ball, like a big pearl with a yellowish aura surrounding it, and in the centre – in the interior – there was a reddish light. [See Rodríguez' sketch, Figure 8.7.) It was a UFO, there's no doubt in my mind about it. It was flying in a south-east to north-east trajectory, and the helicopters were chasing it.'

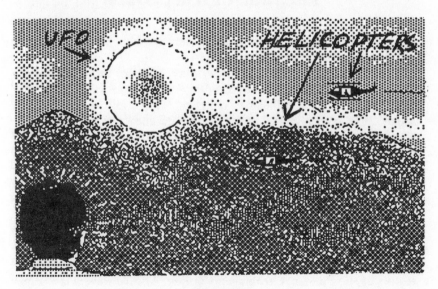

Figure 8:7.

111

We asked Rodríguez if he could give us an estimate of the UFO's dimensions.

'That thing was as big as 747 airliner, compared to the helicopters,' he replied. 'And the strangest thing was that it was flying totally noiselessly.'

Zahíra Milagros Larregoity, a 13-year-old girl, was another witness to the incident. 'I was coming to Mario's house to ask for some ice,' she said, 'and suddenly I saw this big ball of yellow light flying overhead noiselessly, and it flew over the mountain and disappeared. Then I saw that there were some helicopters chasing it in the same direction. It was a very beautiful light . . .'

The mountain over which this happened is north of the Bairoa Park and Mirador Bairoa urban developments area, and on previous occasions other UFOs have been observed over that same mountain. I myself was witness to one such sighting in November 1981.

The helicopters involved must have been either from the Puerto Rico National Air Guard or from Roosevelt Roads, but neither of these bases would acknowledge such an incident or their participation in the chase. An interesting detail is that the object seen by Rodríguez is similar to the one seen by José Antonio Valdés, his wife Matilde and the military officer in Guavate, Cayey, some months before.

'Electrical' UFO in Carraízo

To give readers some idea of the significance of the situation in Puerto Rico, I would like to describe a shocking incident that happened in March 1991, in the town of Trujillo Alto.

It was the night of 17 March. Everything was quiet and normal in the Carraízo sector of the town of Trujillo Alto. But just after midnight, there was a sudden explosion of lights, colours and a strange loud sound. For many miles around, the darkness of night became illuminated with a light of incredible proportions. At a distance, it could be seen that the sky had acquired an intense turquoise-blueish colour, and at the same time the electrical power failed in several sectors miles away. Everything was illuminated with a very bright greenish light that suddenly changed to orange light. To add a spectacular touch to all this, a bright white ray of light could be seen projecting itself up into the sky, moving from left to right and vice versa, in a uniform, fanlike motion.

This display was seen by thousands of witnesses for miles around Trujillo Alto. Those nearer to the area, and those in high areas in the sectors of Rio Piedras, Carolina and Trujillo Alto, however, saw something even more spectacular. Directly over an electrical power substation, located just behind the El Conquistador urban development, in Carraízo sector, hovered an immense circular UFO, motionless in mid-air and radiating a great and intense light. Many residents of El Conquistador could see how the substation's electrical energy was being attracted by the strange craft above it. Something like an energy 'curtain' could be seen around the substation, and in that curtain it was possible to see the electrical energy flowing into the underside of the huge object.

Within a few minutes, people began to congregate in the area of the substation, while many others called the police or radio stations to report what was happening, or asking for information about the phenomenon they were observing. One of those present, Josué Marrero, described the scene as like something out of a Steven Spielberg film. 'This was huge,' he reported, 'and the light was as intense as sunlight. It was as if night had suddenly become day. And the electrical energy was going up in a wall of sparks, and electrical discharges going upwards. I've never seen anything like that! I even had to take my eyes away from it; the light was too bright and hurt them.' José Miranda, another witness, who lives in Diego Velázquez Avenue in El Conquistador, stated:

'What I saw when I looked through the back window after the bright light engulfed everything, was something of which I could see only about a fourth of its size and shape. It was motionless there in the sky, and to me it was something round, some strange type of craft with a shiny nickel-like metallic round edge. At the underside – that is, the side I could see most of – following that edge was a thin line of phosphorescent green light, and next to that one, more to the centre, there was another one of blue-violet phosphorescent light, and at its centre that very powerful bright white light, like a welding light. I saw that as well as electrical rays – discharges going up, in colours – something like that. All this area was as if in daylight, and the light changed from green to blue to orange. I saw it up there for about 30 seconds ... and when the electrical power failed completely that thing shot away to the north at great speed. I ran to the front window but it had already gone.

'My wife, who had seen part of what happened, was screaming in her bed, because we had never seen a craft as big as that one so close and hanging there over our houses. That thing easily would have covered most of this area because it was so big – it was enormous. To me, what I saw was an alien craft, something not normal – something not from this planet.'

113

José's neighbour, Rafael Benítez, a psychologist we know personally, described the scene as follows:

'When I looked out of the rear window, because everything was as if in daylight and the electrical power was gone, I saw this thing with three very bright light sources underneath its centre. I also saw something like a wall of electrical rays going upwards, like thousands of minute electrical capillaries – thin electrical discharges going up – and you could hear a "chh, chh, chh" sound, rather like when you hear static electricity. The wall of electricity was wider at its base and as it went up to that thing in the air it became thinner. Surrounding the object was something like a cloud.' (See Figure 8.8).

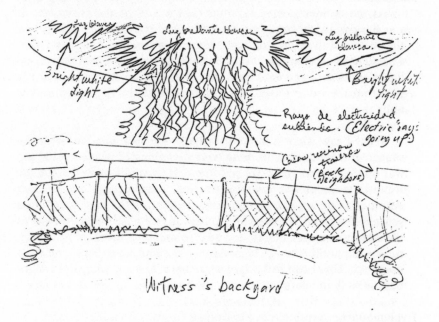

Figure 8:8.

'That thing I saw was not anything I know of from earthly technology. The lights were so intense, like spotlights shining downwards, but really intense and blinding. To me, what I saw was an alien craft that visited us, absorbed the station's electrical energy, then charged whatever they wanted to recharge in their ship – maybe they had an energy problem – then left.'

Danny Rodríguez, a young man who lives next to the substation, also saw the incredible light effects when the system shorted, but unfortunately he did not look up above his house, so missed seeing the object. But he remembers clearly that after the incident, he could see for several minutes a strange green phosphorescent ray of light coming down from the sky in the north-west at a 45-degree angle towards the substation. 'It was like a powerful torch beam coming from the sky, and it stood there for some minutes,' he said.

Genaro Bigas, another neighbour who lives in the Diego Velázquez Avenue, explained that when he went to his balcony to see what was happening, he saw an object extending over the roof. It was 'like a huge semicircle of about 180 degrees,' he said, 'standing there in the air over our houses.'

'At the moment I saw it, it was rather dark on the underside but was flashing bright orange lights from its sides all around it. That was the source of the light which was illuminating everything here. There was something solid up there, because you could see some orange lights on its rim, and then above it you could see the clouds and sky, but from the rim inwards you could see a solid dark surface. Then, after that, some very bright white lights appeared on its underside in the centre.

'What I saw is consistent with what is called traditionally a flying saucer. It was huge, as big as most of this urban residential area, but it was up there, motionless. How could that be, just standing in the air? It must have been very heavy. It was just incredible, but we all saw it. Another thing was that while it was up there, you could feel like a sensation of heat. When it left, we all felt a refreshing gust of wind at the same moment. I'm sorry I didn't come out to have a better look at it, but maybe it was my protective instinct that prevented me from doing so. This I can say: If it was something alien, it wasn't hostile, because it didn't harm us, except for the damage at the substation.'

Evelyn Suárez, a resident in the Colinas de Fairview urbanization area, also in Trujillo but some 3 miles away from where the incident occurred, was able to see the object suspended over the El Conquistador sector.

'What I saw was enormous. It was round and its outer metal structure looked like copper, with an orange luminosity all around it. If you saw the movie *Starman*, the UFO in it was rather like a huge globe of red-orange light with many lights: it was something like that. It also had green and other coloured lights around it, and I'm sure that there were other smaller luminous objects all around, close to it.

115

That was a hell of a craft. I never expected to see anything like that – ever.'

José and Sonia Adorno, who live on the 15th floor of Los Cedros condominium in Trujillo Alto, were also witnesses to this extraordinary event, as Sonia reported:

'It was about 12.20 a.m. and suddenly everything became very bright. When we looked out, we saw something very big and round in the air, surrounded by some kind of cloud. There was a bright yellowish-blueish light going up from the ground to something like a huge platform which was up in the air over El Conquistador. It was rather round and a little flattened at the top with yellow-orange light all around it.

'I was frightened by what I saw, but my husband said it was nothing, maybe only a malfunctioning electrical transformer. But it was not that; it was something weird. Then it flew away to the north and disappeared at great speed. It was huge. I would compare its size with that of the Trujillo Alto Plaza Shopping Centre, but of course, that was at the distance I was seeing it . . .'

Ramses Díaz, a youngster who lives in the Cuidad Universitaria urbanization, was yet another witness, together with his brother. 'It was luminous, something huge in a cloud, a big ball of orange light with many smaller lights on it,' he commented. 'I called the National Weather Service in Isla Verde, and their forecaster told me there was no electrical storm that night and that they couldn't explain what the people were describing . . .'

Many residents in the Covadonga residential area in Trujillo Alto observed this incredible sight, including Elizabeth Torres. 'It was beautiful!' she said. 'It was a big flying saucer. When everything became illuminated, we came out and saw that big object there in the sky, hovering motionless over the mountains over Carraízo. It was a very big orange saucer, with orange light and smaller lights changing colours all around it. Beautiful! All this area was full of people watching it.'

Luis Rodríguez, a security guard who patrols the premises of a company in Carolina, next to the Travenol company, stated that he saw the object as it was flying over very fast to the west, towards Trujillo Alto. It was huge, he said, like an orange ball of light with many smaller coloured lights on it, and it seemed to come from the west. 'I still get nervous when I think about what I saw,' he commented.

Some 6 miles from Carraízo, Enzo Rizzo, who lives in Los Almos condominium, Rio Piedras, observed 'the object and its great luminosity, as well as a series of very strong beams of white light coming out from the top of it and projecting up into space while moving in a fan-like motion. It was an incredible sight, something out of this world.'

Aftermath

The following day, several brigades from the Puerto Rico Authority of Electrical Energy began to repair the $355,000 worth of damage at the substation, which included burned-out electrical poles, several high-voltage power lines and a number of burned-out transformers. (See Plates 8.9–10) We interviewed two supervisors and engineers and asked what had happened.

'We still can't explain what caused all this damage,' said Orlando Lozada. 'There was no reason for this to happen as it did. Firstly, there was a very powerful short circuit due to an apparent contact between two high-voltage lines which were far enough from each other to prevent that from happening. But it happened somehow.'

Technically, his answer already implied that there was a mysterious factor involved in whatever happened. But there was another question: If what occurred was a short circuit, as explained officially, why where the systems not turned off by the safety systems that prevent this from happening, instead of allowing the electrical energy to continue to flow as it did for several minutes, increasing the amperage to an astounding level?

'This station has an automatic system to prevent that,' replied engineer José Luis García. 'As soon as there is an overload it is supposed to cut off the energy flow. If it fails to do this, there is an alternative one that cuts off the energy. However, what happened here was of such a magnitude that neither emergency system responded. This caused an extreme energy overload, and the energy level went to infinite. That explains the damage here.'

'What happened just wasn't natural,' another engineer told us. 'There is no explanation for how things happened here last night.'

A senior supervisor in the Authority of Electrical Energy revealed confidentially that the controllers or 'raisers' failed to function at the substation. 'This type of failure is not common, especially since the equipment is well maintained,' he told us. 'We call these types of discharges "shootouts", and in this case, because of the raisers failing to operate, we call it just that ... But in Puerto Rico there are many "shootouts" due to unknown and mysterious causes. Something that could explain this is what an employee told me, pertaining to similar

117

occurrences in Arecibo [about 40 miles from San Juan]. He explained that he saw when a flying saucer came down and began absorbing power from another substation there in Cruce Dávila, in Barceloneta, next to the Abbot Pharmaceutical Laboratories compound, with effects similar to those seen in Trujillo Alto.'

Everything indicates that a huge UFO was really observed by numerous witnesses in Trujillo Alto and neighbouring communities; a UFO that somehow apparently controlled the substation emergency systems to prevent them from cutting off the power flow. The subsequent great overload was apparently what this object or craft was looking for, maybe to recharge some internal systems, or for something else that we cannot even imagine at present.

Of particular significance is the fact that to date more than 100 witnesses to this spectacular incident – some as far as 10 miles apart from each other – have come forward, all of them giving similar descriptions of the object. In addition, the National Weather Service confirmed that there were no electrical storms that night in the vicinity of Puerto Rico, this being the official explanation by the Government and the Authority of Electrical Energy officers who tried to cover up the incident. To the residents of El Conquistador and the Carraízo community, one thing is clear: they are sure that they were visited by an alien craft, possibly of extraterrestrial origin.

Peripheral Phenomena

In addition to this incident, several other phenomena were reported in the vicinity. For example, a number of residents in El Conquistador with ceiling fans in their homes reported that the fans' arms bent upwards while the UFO was above their homes, as if attracted by a strong magnetic force. Other witnesses say that their table fans began circling backwards, returning to normal after the UFO departed. Some witnesses' telephone answering machines began releasing the recorded messages of their own accord. A lady resident in El Conquistador who has a metal plate in her head due to brain surgery stated that she felt a very sharp pain in her head while the UFO was above. Finally, on the day after the incident, a 17-year-old girl who had observed the UFO began to levitate, witnessed by her mother.

Another interesting factor was the behaviour of animals in the area. Many roosters and dogs, normally noisy, remained totally silent and subdued all that night and until late the following day.

Plate 6.2. This photograph, taken near Frunze, USSR, on 21 September 1990, shows an area of burning grass following the sighting and possible landing of a large UFO, witnessed by three officers of the Militia.

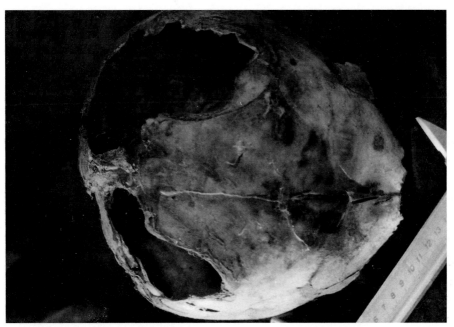

Plate 6.3. According to Dr S. Begaliev, head physician of the Panfilovski Central Regional Hospital, this skull could have come from a creature with a highly developed intellect, but of no known terrestrial species. The skull was discovered in the region of Susamir, Kirgiszkaya, USSR, following many reports of UFOs and 'Bigfoot'-type creatures in October 1990.

Plate 6.4. Aleksandr Dolotov (right) stands at the spot in Lermontovski Prospekt, Leningrad, where he encountered and was possibly abducted by four alien beings on the night of 17 June 1990. On the left is Dr Rita Dolotov and Nikolai Lebedev.

Plate 6.5. Nikolai Lebedev stands at the spot in Izmailovski Prospekt, Leningrad, 600 metres away from the encounter, where Dolotov was later discovered unconscious by soldiers.

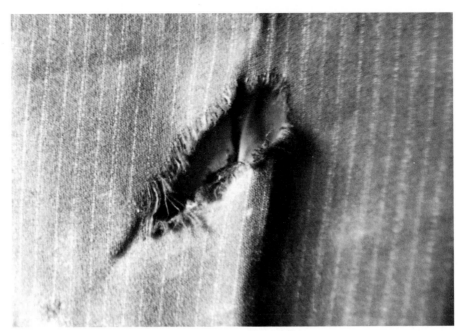

Plate 6.6. One of the unexplainable holes in Aleksandr Dolotov's trousers, discovered after the encounter.

Plate 7.1. The famous 'road shot', taken by Ed Walters at Gulf Breeze, Florida, on 12 January 1988. This photograph has been enlarged and light-enhanced by Bob Oechsler. The craft is 14-15 ft. in diameter. (© Ed Walters)

Plate 8.1. The El Yunque mountain in the National Caribbean Rain Forest, Puerto Rico, where Rosa Dávila and her neighbours saw the UFO and jet fighters encounter on 4 July 1989. (© Enigma!)

Plate 8.2. A U.S. Navy F-18 Hornet, of the type involved in the UFO chase near the U.S. Army base at Fort Allen, Juana Díaz, in Puerto Rico, 18 July 1990. (© Timothy Good)

Plate 8.3. Miguel Figueroa, one of the witnesses to the incident involving five alien creatures seen in the Cabo Rojo area of Puerto Rico on 31 August 1990. (© Enigma!)

Plate 8.4. Bridge over which the aliens jumped into a creek, heading in the direction of the Laguna Cartagena. (© Enigma!)

Plate 8.5. Photo of Luis Diodonet and a superimposed drawing of the UFO he saw next to the aerostat installation at Oliveras, Puerto Rico, on 17 August 1990. (© Enigma!)

Plate 8.7. Zahíra Milagros Larregoity, who also witnessed the UFO/helicopters encounter. (© Enigma!)

Plate 8.6. Mario Orlando Rodríguez, one of the witnesses to the ball of light chased by helicopters over Caguas, Puerto Rico, on 19 December 1990. (© Enigma!)

Plate 8.8. Genaro Bigas, one of over 100 witnesses to an incident in Trujillo Alto, Puerto Rico, on 17 March 1991, when a huge circular UFO hovered low over the electric substation, causing extensive damage. (© Enigma!)

Plates 8.9. & 8.10. Burned-out transformers and electrical equipment costing
$355,000 in losses, following a UFO incident in Trujillo Alto, Puerto Rico.

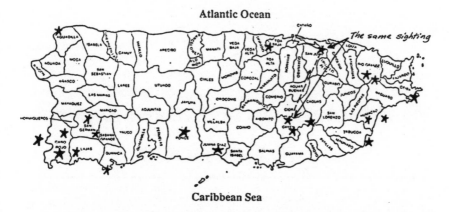

Figure 8:9. The stars on the map show the places in Puerto Rico where there have been UFO/jet-fighter encounters or chases.

Many questions remain unanswered about all the important incidents presented in this report; incidents that are only a fraction of the plethora of such cases. But without a doubt, these events indicate that the UFO phenomenon is very close to Puerto Rico's everyday reality. Every day, I receive more reports of UFO/jet chases from credible witnesses all around the island. Just before finishing this article, I received two more, which I hope to publish in next year's *UFO Report*.

Due to the amount of activity here, I sometimes wonder if Puerto Rico has been selected as a place where open contact with an alien species will be tested, to check on the psychological and sociological reactions of such a contact. We must remember that Puerto Rico is a US territorial possession, and it is very possible that 'someone' could have selected the island for such a test because it is under US jurisdiction, and this would provide for a close scrutiny by the Government on the developing situation, with the advantage of not risking the mainland's citizens and any unforseen effect that might come out of the experiment.

In the US and abroad, many believe that an agreement exists between the US Government and a certain species of aliens. Although there is no specific proof, there is a lot of circumstantial evidence that in my view tends to imply just that. In most of the incidents described here, the relationship between the UFO situation and the Roosevelt Roads Naval Station – a principal US military base – is evident.

Because of this, as well as the increasing number of UFO/jet chase reports, I ask myself: Are the jet fighters really chasing the UFOs? Or are they 'escorting' them . . . ?

9

World Round-up of Selected Reports

TIMOTHY GOOD

Although certain correlations can be made, no firm conclusions of a statistical nature should be drawn from the following reports, which I have selected from hundreds, covering the period of May 1990 to June 1991.

The preponderance of reports from Great Britain, Puerto Rico, USA and the USSR, for example, should not lead to the assumption that more sightings have occurred in these countries. The shortage or lack of reports from other countries (such as India) is probably due to such factors as a reluctance to report, a dearth of researchers or journalists, and poor communications. In addition, I have to admit that I receive few foreign-language journals and newspaper cuttings (or translations thereof); a fault I hope to remedy in future.

As well as providing some interesting reports, my intention here is to emphasize the massive scale of the phenomenon, which is too frequently overlooked.

Those requiring further information should contact the reporters, researchers, newspapers and journals concerned, since I am unable to vouch for the accuracy of all these necessarily condensed accounts.

---

1 May 1990: Runcorn, Cheshire, UK

Cycling home to Murdishaw at 22.15, a man was startled by the sight of a low-flying object. 'It flew past right in front of me,' he told reporter Carla Flynn. 'I've been spotting aircraft for years and I know this definitely wasn't any aeroplane: it didn't travel like one and it was certainly going too fast to be one.'

The witness (Tony) described the UFO as circular in shape with a dome on top, creamy white in colour and illuminated. 'It was travelling at tremendous speed and in a straight line, but with a sort of bobbing movement. It was also very low – or appeared to be very low. It was also silent: there was no noise coming from it at all, and it was heading in the direction of Frodsham.' (Carla Flynn, *Runcorn World*, 4 May 1990)

5 May 1990: Widnes, Cheshire, UK
At 03.50 (or 04.40), Mr J was awoken by 'a sort of vibrating, rushing' noise which seemed to sweep along the road and past his window. It took some 3 minutes to pass and caused the window and a window downstairs to shake violently, he told investigator Peter Hough. After 5 minutes, it returned from the opposite direction, sweeping past and again shaking the house. Minutes later, it returned for a third time. Mr J now had enough courage to sit on the edge of the bed, and through the curtains saw a huge white ball of light just above the road. It seemed to hover for several seconds, then as the witness got up to open the curtains it shot skyward and vanished. The noise ceased.

'The most baffling feature of the case (for which we mooted some type of road sweeping machine as a possible answer),' writes Jenny Randles, 'is that *nobody* heard the object other than Mr J. Neither the police nor local press had reports. Mr J even called the local taxi firm to see if any of their night drivers had heard it. But no . . .' Another similar incident was reported on 27 June in Norfolk, as we shall learn. (Investigator: Peter Hough, Manchester UFO Research Association (MUFORA); report by Jenny Randles, *Northern UFO News*, No. 145, October 1990)

18/19 May: Kairma, near Frunze, Kirgizskaya, USSR
At 21.40, a mother and her son claimed to have seen alien creatures with glowing suits and three claw-like fingers to each hand. Later in the night a strong droning sound was heard, the local power supply was affected, and at 00.30 (19 May) a huge red disk-shaped object flew over Kairma, with bright beams of light shining down. At 13.21, a group of grey-coloured discs was seen flying over Frunze (see pp.65–6).

19 May 1990: Warrior, Alabama, USA
A woman driving to work was confronted by six huge lights approaching slowly at treetop level. She halted, at which point the object hesitated, then moved at jogging speed over her truck and into the distance until lost from view. As it passed overhead, she sensed a vibration. The vehicle was described as at least house-sized and consisting of two sections (Figure 9:1). The front section was trapezoidal, behind which was a broad, outwardly-angled fuselage and blunt rear. Along the fuselage was a strip composed of hundreds of red, green and blue lights. The duration of the sighting was estimated as six to eight minutes. (Investigator: Todd Pierce; summarized by Dan Wright, *MUFON UFO Journal*, No. 270, October 1990)

(front view)

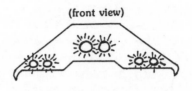

(bottom view)

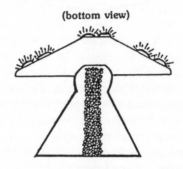

Figure 9:1.

24 May 1990: North Huntingdon, Pennsylvania, USA
A woman was walking her dog at 23.00 when she saw a dark, delta-shaped object, somewhat larger than a commercial prop-driven aircraft, with nine large white lights extending around the two leading edges. The rear edge was reminiscent of a boomerang curvature. The vehicle hovered 300 feet above the ground near powerlines, then left quickly and was lost from view. The witness sensed a vibration during the sighting, which lasted for about 30 seconds. (Investigator: Wayne Willis; summarized by Dan Wright *MUFON UFO Journal*, No. 270, October 1990)

28 May 1990: Kirwan, Queensland, Australia
At 02.30, amateur astronomer John Bentley was standing outside facing east, anticipating a view of Austin's Comet, when he saw a fast-moving object travelling from north to south (Figure 9:2). No noise was heard. (Compiled by Phillip Frola, *ACUFOS Reports Digest*, No. 38, March/April 1991, published by the Australian Centre for UFO Studies)

29 May 1990: Kairma, near Frunze, Kirgizskaya, USSR
Three women at a garage office on a collective farm reported seeing a strange creature with glowing eyes, no nose and a slit for a mouth. From

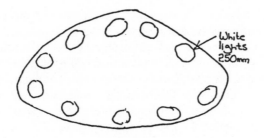

Figure 9:2.

another viewpoint, two boys claimed to have seen a 'flying saucer' land, and one boy (the other ran away) reported seven 'pilots', one 3 metres tall, the rest about a metre and a half, who divided into two groups. The first group gathered samples from the ground in a bizarre fashion, while the second group headed for the garage. Later, the boy saw the women running from the office. After 15 minutes, the beings allegedly returned to their craft, took off, then landed not far from a repair shop! (see pp.66–8).

17 June 1990: Leningrad, USSR
A possible abduction was reported by A. Dolotov (see pp.70–71).

21 June 1990: Pensacola, Florida, USA
Through a window at a business establishment, a woman noticed an unusual low cloud in the near distance at 14.15, and called it to the attention of her four companions. Momentarily, a large silvery disc emerged from the cloud and hovered. The bottom of the object was described as a rimmed crescent lined with apparent portholes, overlying which was a 'straw hat-like' crown. The surface reflected the sun's glare. After three minutes, the witnesses' attention was momentarily distracted to discuss the sighting, and when they looked back, it had gone. (Investigator: Joe Barron; summarized by Dan Wright, *MUFON UFO Journal*, No. 272, December 1990)

22 June 1990: Near Williams Lake, British Columbia, Canada
Driving home from work just after midnight, Debbie Meldrum encountered a large, bright orange, saucer-shaped object. The bottom of the saucer was lighter in colour than the rest, with small holes that she believes could have been windows. She tried to take photos, but the light coming from the object set the light meter in her camera off the

scale so she gave up. 'It was so bright, it blinded me when I looked through the camera' she reported.

Meldrum said that her right arm, then her left, started to get numb. Soon her face felt numb too. At that point, she decided to leave. 'After that it started to move. I didn't know, but I thought it was coming towards me.' The object followed the river that runs parallel to the road, keeping pace with Meldrum, who left in a hurry and eventually lost sight of the object. (*Tribune*, Williams Lake, B.C., Canada, 27 June 1990)

22 June 1990: Guavate, Puerto Rico
Several witnesses, including a military officer, observed a 'ball of light' pursued by jet fighters.' (see pp.101–103).

27 June 1990: Wicklewood, Wymondham, Norfolk, UK
Mr B was awoken at 00.18 by his three-year-old son crying. It was a dry, hot and humid night, with no wind. After settling the child, Mr and Mrs B heard a 'very distinctive sound that I would liken to a large object moving at high speed through the air – a sort of whooshing effect,' Mr B told Peter Hough. 'I was also aware of a very bright light briefly illuminating the room through the curtains – much brighter than car lights.'

Both witnesses recalled hearing similar sounds before, but without lights. Although the local press and police had no reports for that night, the police did comment that their patrols 'had witnessed similar phenomena on past occasions'. (Investigator: Peter Hough, MUFORA; report by Jenny Randles, *Northern UFO News*, No. 145, October 1990)

5 July 1990: Pensacola Beach, Florida, USA
Bob and Mary Oechsler witnessed extraordinary luminous phenomena on the horizon, which were captured on film. (see pp.96–7).

7 July 1990: Anhui, Jiangsu and Shandong Provinces, China
Numerous witnesses reported sighting an extraordinary cluster of up to thirty-two star-like objects, in a regularly changing pattern (see pp.50–51).

9 July 1990: Shawan District, Sichuan Province, China
A 'flying saucer', eventually dividing into two identical saucers, performed a series of manoeuvres in front of a number of witnesses (see pp.51–2).

13 July 1990: Kingston-upon-Hull, Humberside, UK
At around 23.00, a woman and her son watched a UFO through binoculars from their home in south-west Hull. The woman told police that the
object was triangular in shape when viewed sideways, with a square rear
end. The UFO emitted bright, constant lights.

According to a police spokesman, the object 'hovered for 30 minutes
and then shot off vertically until it disappeared from view. Flames were
observed coming from the rear . . .' (*Hull Daily Mail*, 14 July 1990)

13 July 1990: Near Manchester, New Hampshire, USA
From her bedroom, a teenager observed a brilliant light rise from, and
hover over, a wetland across the road a few hundred feet away.
Momentarily, she realized this was the forward light of a tapered cylindrical object as it rotated to reveal its length.

A series of square lights or windows were equally spaced across the
midsection of its dark metallic grey surface. At one end appeared to be a
horizontal cable, at the end of which was a red light. The object
proceeded laterally until lost beyond a line of trees. Duration of the
sighting was less than a minute. (Investigator: Ruth Michaud; summarized by Dan Wright, *MUFON UFO Journal*, No. 274, February 1991)

18 July 1990: Fort Allen, Juana Díaz, Puerto Rico
A military officer at the US Army Reserve base reported the observation
of a disk-like object, pursued by jet fighters (see pp.103–105).

26 July 1990: Pewsey Down, Wiltshire, UK
While examining a large 'pictogram' in daytime at Milk Hill, Pewsey
Down, a couple was astonished to observe a small shiny object which they
filmed with a video camera (see pp.5–6).

28 July 1990: Brisbane, Queensland, Australia
While travelling home at 21.20, Amanda Green and her three children
sighted a saucer-shaped object with a dome on top, hovering to the left of
them at Thornsland, Brisbane. It was white and flashing red, green, white
and yellow lights. Mrs Green was obliged to drive quite close to the object
in order to reach home, almost passing right underneath it. On arrival,
the object was still visible. Hoping that her husband might see it, she ran
into the house, only to discover when they returned outside that the
object had disappeared. The children later complained of sore eyes.
(Investigators: Phillip Frola and Sheryl Demichelis; *UFO Encounter*, No.
137, October/November 1990, published by UFO Research Queensland)

30 July 1990: Boscombe Down, Wiltshire, UK

At 22.30, physiotherapist Jane Manning-Philips observed a large flying machine heading over her home towards Boscombe Down. 'What I saw must have been a UFO,' she said. 'I have never seen anything like it and we have a lot of strange MoD aircraft flying over here. It made a terrible noise, like it was about to crash. It was ugly, and really quite frightening.

'Then I saw this strange cylinder-shaped object which was flying vertically. That was what amazed me most – it was upright. It had two very big red lights at the top and bottom and an orangey-yellow light either side in the middle. I watched it fly over Porton school towards Highpost and then round to Boscombe Down, where it seemed to disappear.' Others reported hearing the unusual noise.

Press Officer Simon Kuczera from the Aeroplane and Armament Experimental Establishment at Boscombe Down later offered the 'solution': the UFO was merely a Boeing 747–400 [the latest type] flying low over the area. British Airways subsequently confirmed that these new aircraft had been flying in the area while training pilots – and on the night in question. 'It was flying low at between 12,000 and 18,000 feet and its navigation lights would have been flashing,' explained Public Affairs Officer Alan Solloway. (*The Avon Advertiser*, 8/15/22 August 1990)

(An altitude of 12,000–18,000 feet can hardly be described as 'low', and I await eagerly the sight of a Boeing 747 flying vertically.)

30 July 1990: Great Yarmouth, Norfolk, UK

Four members of a family at Hopton, near Great Yarmouth, observed a red object 'like a rear light' with a ring surrounding it during the night, which appeared to be descending. The following morning, a Cropfield Circle, surrounded by ten equidistant smaller Circles, was discovered by a farm manager in the area where the object had been seen.

(This report was passed to me by David Dane, the well known Norfolk-based artist who has conducted numerous investigations into the Cropfield Circles.)

4 August 1990: North Walsham, Norfolk, UK

A farming family at Knapton, near North Walsham, was alerted at 23.30 by the sound of all the dogs in the area barking, following by a noise similar to that of a power-saw cutting through timber. The farmer's wife, having gone upstairs to the bedroom, saw a bright orange globe with a line of lights slowly rotating on the outer edge. She called her husband and son, and all three watched as the object appeared to descend into Witton Wood. The lights then disappeared, but suddenly the family saw a huge fork of lightning much higher.

On the following morning, the farmer discovered that the batteries on his tractor had gone flat. Furthermore, typical Cropfield Circles were found in a barley field on the farm – for the second time that summer.

(This report was given to me within a few days of the event by David Dane.)

August 1990: St Mary's Loch, Selkirk, Scotland
John Hay, an artist living in a fairly isolated area on the Scottish borders, observed a curious flying object one Saturday morning at around 08.00.

'I looked out of the Velux window above my bed in our attic bedroom and saw a totally silent craft flying overhead. It was a beautiful morning, with hardly a birdsong to disturb the peace. The object flying over looked a bit like a rugby ball with pointed ends and stubby wings on either side at the mid-position.

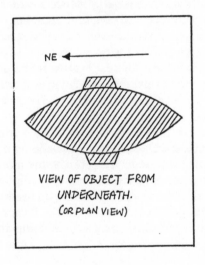

Figure 9:3.

'Everything seemed totally normal except for this odd vehicle, and I had to try hard not to rationalize the object away as being a balloon or airship of some kind. However, there was no wind to drive it along on its steady course, and no engine noise. I must emphasize that the loch

127

is incredibly quiet (except at lambing time) and any noise seems intrusive. We are however on a training route for Tornado and Jaguar pilots, which fact helps me to gauge the height and speed of the vehicle I saw, although it is of course difficult when there is nothing to relate to except sky.

'My son was awake and watching the craft too, and we agree that it seemed to be flying at about 400 feet in a north-easterly direction at perhaps 70 m.p.h. Because I somehow couldn't accept the strangeness of this vehicle and was determined not to create a fanciful "UFO", I stopped watching, but my son, who was looking out of another window, further along in the roof of the cottage, kept on following it . . .

'On being distracted by me he looked away, however, and by the time that he looked back at it (a matter of seconds) the object had gone! He is a bright boy, and maintains that the craft, on the course it was following and at the speed at which it was travelling, could not have passed behind the hills around the loch . . . and he therefore feels that it simply *disappeared*.

'The craft was a pale greenish/grey colour, had no visible markings of any kind, made no sound, had no visible means of propulsion, left no vapour trail or exhaust smoke, and moved at a constant speed . . . There were no lights visible or windows that we could see, and no cabin underneath as in an airship . . . I have seen quite a number of advertising balloons and airships, and this wasn't one of those . . . such airships are usually very noisy!' (John Hay, *Flying Saucer Review*, Vol. 36, No. 2, 1991)

15 August 1990: Babinda, Queensland, Australia
At 20.00, two people witnessed a large, bright moon-sized object, oval in shape with smaller lights along its circumference (Figure 9:4) hovering in the sky. Although the object was brightly lit, the stars could still be seen through it. No noise was heard during the sighting, which lasted three minutes. (Compiled by Phillip Frola, *ACUFOS Reports Digest*, No. 38, March/April 1991, published by the Australian Centre for UFO Studies)

17 August 1990: Oliveras, Puerto Rico
Several witnesses observed a UFO shaped like a 'witch's hat' (see pp.109–10).

22 August 1990: Workington, Cumbria, UK
While walking his dog at 02.30, businessman Roy Daugherty claims to have witnessed a large ball of light hovering close to the Westland Hotel

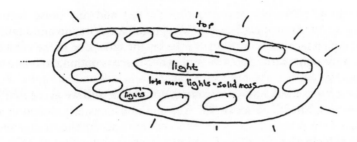

Figure 9:4.

in Workington. 'It was a great big mass of light and it pulled down from the sky in front of me. It hovered there for about half a minute and I just kind of froze looking at it, and so did my dog. It seemed like it was looking at us and then pulled off horizontally at great speed,' reported Mr Dougherty, who is chief executive of the Westland Group which owns the hotel. He described the object, which was shrouded in the light, as a rounded structure some 60–80 feet off the ground. (*West Cumberland Times*, Cockermouth, 24 August 1990)

31 August 1990: Cabo Rojo, Puerto Rico
A number of witnesses encountered five strange creatures, who subsequently jumped over a bridge and headed in the direction of the Laguna Cartagena (see pp.105–9).

2 September 1990: Murmansk, USSR
TASS news agency reported that Soviet anti-aircraft defences monitored the flight of a UFO, adding that the brightly illuminated object looked like an airship and flew at an altitude of 15 miles from the Barents Sea to the Kola Peninsula. (*Kent Evening Post*, 3 September 1990)

13 September 1990: Kuybyshev/Samara, Siberia, USSR
Following the tracking of a large flying object, military personnel observed the landing of a black triangular-shaped craft at the long-range radar tracking station near Kuybyshev. The UFO allegedly destroyed one of the radar posts, and two sentries who temporarily disappeared experienced time loss (see pp.73–7).

16 September 1990: West Jordan, Utah, USA
At 19.52, Denise and Stephen Haddenham, together with their two children, observed a silver, disc-shaped object as they were driving

home from a restaurant. Stopping the car, the witnesses watched the UFO for about 30 seconds before it disappeared swiftly behind a grove of tall trees. The object – estimated to be the size of a yo-yo held at arm's length – appeared to be a grey metallic disc with a dome on top reflecting the sun. A shimmer of air seemed to follow the object, like heat rising from a hot surface. (Investigator: Mildred Biesele, *MUFON UFO Journal*, No. 277, May 1991)

21 September 1990: Frunze, Kirgizskaya, USSR
Three militia officers reported encountering a huge flying saucer which apparently landed, leaving a large area of burned grass (see pp.68–69).

24 September 1990: Near Luton, Bedfordshire, UK
Bob Boyd, Chairman of the Plymouth UFO Research Group, was travelling on a coach from Heathrow to Sunderland when at about 11.15 he spotted a brilliant white cigar-shaped object rising above the trees (Figure 9:5).

Figure 9:5.

'My first thoughts were that it must be an advertising balloon, but it wasn't of the usual type ... It had quite pointed ends and at its thickest points it was also quite pointed. The object was about three-quarters of an inch long at arm's length. When it rose up it was a brilliant white all over (the sun was shining on it), but after it levelled off there was a pronounced shadow on the lower half. I could clearly see this object. I had been watching it for some 30 seconds by now, and decided I could not identify it.

'I thought the proximity to Luton Airport counted against it being an advertising balloon, even though it remained at a low altitude during the sighting, and it seemed to be in fairly open country ... Its method of ascent was not that of a balloon. I already had my camera on the seat beside me, so picked it up and went to take a shot, but immediately the object was hidden by a hill. It was 45 seconds or so before I saw it again.

'I realized, when looking through the viewfinder, how much the bus was shaking: I knew that there was too much vibration for a shutter speed of 125th, so reset it to 1000th of a second on f5.6 . . . The object came into view again and I quickly took a shot before it was hidden again. I then took shots whenever it was visible . . .

'On checking a map later, I estimated the object to have been somewhere between Sundon and Harlington. I thought it was about half a mile from me when first seen . . . The sighting lasted 5 or 6 minutes, though it was only visible for about a third of that time. I have no idea if the object was moving [after the initial ascent] . . . '

(Report and sketch by Bob Boyd. Unfortunately, the object shown on the photographs is too small for reproduction here.)

27 September 1990: Earth orbit
Cosmonauts G. Manokov and G. Strekalov, on board the space station Mir, reported sighting a huge silvery UFO after they had passed over Newfoundland (see pp.72–3).

27 September 1990: Clacton-on-Sea/Point Clear, Essex, UK
At 22.45, while walking her dog along the Clacton seafront, Mrs B observed a large, 'boomerang-shaped' object, estimated to be over 200 feet in size, moving slowly and silently over the sea on an east to west course, apparently parallel to the coast. Mrs B estimated the object to be approximately half a mile out to sea and at about 1,000 feet altitude.

The object had one large white light to the front and centre, with four other smaller white lights on each side of the central large light. After it had passed ahead of her, Mrs B noticed about eighteen red lights to the rear of the craft, as well as an array of other lights to the middle of the object, the colours including blue, green, amber and yellow. The sky was dark and starless, with no people around – unusual for that time of night. The sighting lasted for about 3 minutes. (*Essex UFO Research Newsletter*, No. 5, January/February 1991)

Two witnesses travelling home from Point Clear at 00.30 were startled by two long red lights swooping towards their car. 'It was travelling at tremendous speed, then it turned silently, almost on the spot, around at a 45-degree angle, then flew off towards a woodland area, where it seemed to land. We did not see it again. It had two very long cherry-red lights, which as [the object] banked gave the appearance of being on the

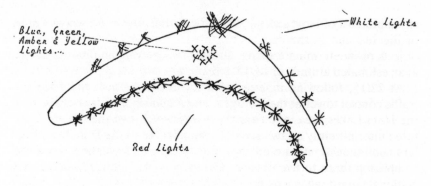

Figure 9:6.

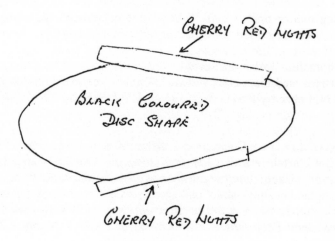

Figure 9:7.

sides of a clearly discernible black disc approximately 200–300 feet across. There was no noise' (Figure 9:7). (*Essex UFO Research Newsletter*, No. 4, November/December 1990)

8 October 1990: Grozniy, Georgia, USSR
Following radar detection of an unknown target at 11.00, Soviet Air Force Major P. Riabishev was sent to intercept and observed two large cigar-shaped objects, which disappeared as he closed in (see p.72).

10 October 1990: Hoyt Lakes, Skibo, Minnesota, USA
At around 21.00, local residents began reporting unusual lights in the

sky south-east of Hoyt Lakes. Two police officers drove to within a mile of the site and in the company of other witnesses observed multiple objects of indeterminate shape, alternately hovering and darting about at an estimated altitude of 10,000 feet or so.

At 22.15, following a series of ambiguous 'returns', the FAA air traffic control tower at the Duluth Airport confirmed radar echoes from the Hoyt Lakes area, and over the next hour or two the targets registered intermittently on two separate radars. One of the Duluth controllers continuously monitored the roughly circular formation, variously comprising three to five objects. The targets also appeared on an Air National Guard radar screen.

A commercial plane flying at 11,000 feet and 40–50 miles west of Hoyt Lakes was notified by the Duluth controllers, and the pilot reported sighting two distinct, steady lights below his altitude and a few miles apart, both described as deep, glowing red. No other conventional aircraft were in the area and no known weather factors accounted for the anomalous radar returns. (Investigators: Bill McNeff and Richard Bauerlein; summarized by Dan Wright, *MUFON UFO Journal*, No. 274, February 1991)

11 October 1990: Bristol, Avon, UK
At 20.00, three people saw a large ball of orange, glowing light hovering over the Hartcliffe area of Bristol. The ball suddenly displayed a red formation of lights and began to move off towards the Dundry Hills. More lights became visible, coloured red, blue and white. Through the lights could be seen a distinct triangular shape. (Tony Dodd, *Quest International: The Journal of UFO Investigation*, Vol. 10, No. 1, 1991)

11 October 1990: Saddleworth Moor, Lancashire, UK
According to police, a Stalybridge man was shaking uncontrollably as he reported two sightings which had occurred at night as he drove along the Holmfirth road close to the Yorkshire/Lancashire border. He described having seen a large, saucer-shaped object, with flashing white lights as he drove into Yorkshire. On his return, a spotlight from the same (?) object shone down on his car. His description matched two independent reports in West Yorkshire, one of which was given by a woman who regularly travels along the same road.

Aviation authorities were not aware of any aircraft in the vicinity around the time of the sightings (from 21.45). (*Oldham Evening Chronicle*, 12 October 1990)

13 October 1990: Thanet, Kent, UK
Several witnesses saw a brilliant white cigar-shaped object pass over-head toward the sea at 22.00. It suddenly stopped dead over the sea and after some minutes shot away at an amazing speed. Two minutes later, a second, identical object passed over their heads and out to sea, also stopping dead. The object hovered for a few minutes before shooting off at high speed. (Tony Dodd, *Quest International: The Journal of UFO Investigation*, Vol. 10, No. 1, 1991)

18 October 1990: Bristol, Avon, UK
At 16.35, Kelly Broom and her friend Rachael Stewart, both ten years old, were playing with a frisbee in a field near their Bristol home when, to their astonishment, the frisbee appeared to 'bounce' back several times, as though it had hit an invisible wall. As Kelly picked up the frisbee, the two girls found themselves inside a kind of transparent 'bubble', unable to get out.

Both girls became very frightened and began to 'bang' on the walls of the bubble in an attempt to escape. Suddenly, a pale yellow mist began to percolate into the bubble from above. Later, both girls described a sensation of pressure which appeared to be pulling them into the mist.

The air at this time was described as being very warm, with both girls experiencing breathing difficulty: in fact, they were only able to breathe while prone inside the bubble. They stated that no sound could be heard from the bubble, and they had to shout very loud in order to hear each other. At one stage, Kelly put her hand on Rachael's coat and described a sensation like that of static electricity.

Rachael later told Kelly that she had seen 'something' inside the bubble, but was unable to remember what it was. Although they were not aware of the exact duration of time spent inside the bubble, it felt like about 4 minutes. Kelly said that one moment they were inside, and the next thing they knew, the bubble had gone. Although a slight wind was blowing at the time, it stopped when the bubble descended over them, yet it started again when the bubble lifted.

Kelly claimed she saw a large flock of blackbirds flying around above the bubble, as if they were unable to fly past it. After the incident, she suffered nightmares for several days: each time, the nightmare was a 're-run' of the experience. Interestingly, at no time was the word 'UFO' mentioned during the interview with investigators from Quest International.

Weather conditions at the time of the incident were fine and dry with a slight wind blowing. No other person could be traced in the area who had witnessed the event or seen any other strange occurrence. Kelly's mother is totally convinced that the girls are telling the truth. (Investigators: Richard Tarr, Marion Norman, Alan and David Neate; summarized by Tony Dodd, *Quest International: The Journal of UFO Investigation*, Vol. 10, No. 1, 1990)

24 October 1990: Louisville, Kentucky, USA
Glancing out of the window of her 12th-floor office at 14.45, a woman noticed a stationary, silvery, flat-bottomed disc below her level, against a backdrop of trees. About 20 feet in diameter, its only feature initially was an upturned rim.

Momentarily, the disc began moving slowly upward and away in an arc, then proceeded back and forth in half-circle paths, alternately displaying its black underside while continually moving further away. The witness was joined by another woman, and then a man, who alone saw a second vehicle – boomerang-shaped – merge in the distance with the first. Perhaps 2 miles distant, the objects suddenly disappeared from view. (Investigator: Burt Monroe; summarized by Dan Wright, *MUFON UFO Journal*, No. 274, February 1991)

29 October 1990: Gloucester/Uxbridge, Middlesex, UK
At 20.15, witnesses in an isolated area of Gloucester saw a large ball of light hovering above high-voltage pylons. The object was changing colour from bright white, to orange, and to red. After at least five minutes, military fighter aircraft were seen heading in the direction of the object. As they approached, the object suddenly disappeared.

At 21.00, a number of witnesses in Uxbridge, Middlesex, observed two very large balls of orange light hovering at treetop level over nearby fields. Suddenly, one of the balls moved slowly away at about 15 m.p.h. and travelled in a big arc before returning to its original position next to the other object. Both objects began to move away slowly when (as in the previous incident) fighter aircraft were seen coming very fast from the opposite direction, passing directly over the area where the lights had been last reported. (Tony Dodd, *Quest International: The Journal of UFO Investigation*, Vol. 10, No. 1, 1991)

30 October 1990: Mount Airy, North Carolina, USA
Irena Stafford was preparing to walk her dogs at 21.30 when she saw a dome-topped object that was 'bigger than a plane or even a zeppelin', hovering near her Mount Airy home. The object made a high-pitched whining sound and had red and green lighted 'portholes' that rotated along its bottom edge, as well as beams of light that sprayed across the sky. During the sighting, the dogs whined, shook, rubbed their ears with

their paws and refused to leave the house. (Investigator: George Fawcett; reported by Emily Smith, *Herald*, Durham, North Carolina)

5 November 1990: Genoa, Italy/North Sea
British Airways Captain Mike D'Alton reported sighting a UFO during the night flight in a Boeing 737 from Rome to Gatwick, describing it as a silver disc with three faint points of light in arrow formation and a fourth light behind it.

Captain D'Alton said the object was visible for about 2 minutes over Genoa. 'I've never seen anything like it before and can't explain what it was. My co-pilot and I called in two cabin crew to see it and then it went out of sight. Ground radar couldn't pick it up, so it must have been travelling at phenomenal speed.' (*Sunday Telegraph*, London/*Sunday Mail*, Glasgow, 11 November 1990)

That same night, another BA captain reported two 'very bright mystifying lights' while flying over the North Sea, and later spoke to an RAF Tornado pilot who, together with another Tornado from the same squadron, had been 'approached by bright lights' which 'formated' on the Tornadoes. The accompanying Tornado pilot was so convinced that they were on a collision course with the lights – apparently nine were seen – that he 'broke away' and took 'violent evasive action'. The formation of UFOs continued 'straight on course and shot off ahead at speed – they were nearly supersonic . . .'

(These incidents were confirmed to Paul Whitehead of the Surrey Investigation Group on Aerial Phenomena via another airline pilot, who had spoken with the BA pilot involved in the North Sea incident, and reported to me by Paul in April 1991. For further details, see *Flying Saucer Review*, Vol. 36, No. 2, 1991. In addition, the following report may provide corroboration.)

5 November 1990: Near Rheindalen, Germany/North Sea
According to a highly placed RAF Germany source, two terrific explosions were heard on two separate occasions at night in the Rheindalen area. After the second explosion (at 22.00) the crew of a Phantom jet reported UFOs heading north in a 'finger' formation.

Separately, two Tornado jets over the North Sea encountered two large round objects, each with five blue lights and several other white lights around the rim. As the Tornadoes closed to investigate, one of the UFOs headed for one of the jets, which had to take violent evasive action to avoid a collision. The two unknowns then headed north until they were out of sight. Nothing showed on the radar screens of the Tornadoes.

5–6 November 1990: Belgium, France, Germany, Italy, Switzerland
Mysterious aerial objects, variously described as orange balls, triangles
and points of light were reported during the night by hundreds of
witnesses in Belgium, France, Germany, Italy and Switzerland. Some
described a moving shape comprising three, five or six brilliant points of
light. Experts in Munich and other countries suggested that a meteorite
or satellite re-entry was to blame.

But in Belgium, dozens reported a triangular object with three lights,
flying slowly and soundlessly to the south-west, and their air force said it
was studying the reports in liaison with neighbouring air forces. Several
crew members of civilian and military planes also sighted UFOs, including a British pilot, who reported four objects flying in formation over
the Ardennes hills in south Belgium.

In France, Jean-Jacques Velasco, director of the Service for the
Investigation of Re-entry Phenomena, said an investigation would be
launched, and confirmed that several airline pilots had reported sightings but that no radar contact was recorded in French airspace. One Air
France pilot told a radio interviewer: 'We were on a flight to Barcelona
at about 33,000 feet at 19.03 hours when we first saw the shape. *It
couldn't have been a satellite [re-entry] because it was there for three or
four minutes'*.

In Italy, six airline pilots reported 'a mysterious and intense white
light' south-east of Turin. Pilots also reported five white smoke trails
nearby. Police in Bavaria were swamped with calls from people reporting streaks of light with fire tails at about 19.00 on 5 November.
(*Glasgow Herald*, 7 November 1990)

6 November 1990: Barham, Victoria, Australia
Mrs Deriece Kopetko, her sister, and three of their children, were
driving through Deniliquin, near Barham, at about 23.30, when they
noticed two red lights in front of them which they assumed to be aircraft
lights, although they made unusual movements in the sky. Mrs Kopetko
said the lights had travelled vertically and horizontally, stopping completely still at certain moments then proceeding to move about in
varying patterns.

After travelling through Deniliquin, approaching Barham, Mrs
Kopetko stopped the car to investigate. She said that one of the lighted
objects landed in a paddock to the left of the car, and hovered with a
blue haze above it. Alarmed, Mrs Kopetko's sister, who had been sitting
in the back seat, turned to the right to avoid looking at the object, only
to be confronted with the other light, which flew over the car at a
distance of about 9–12 metres.

Mrs Kopetko said she had wound down her window to watch the light as it had travelled above the car and noted that it had been completely silent. It appeared to be diamond-shaped with four lights; a red and white light at the front, and a yellow and a bluish-green light at its triangular point. She said the end of the diamond did not have a light, and was in darkness. The object then almost instantaneously moved to join the other light in the paddock.

After having driven on, Mrs Kopetko and her family watched as the moving light travelled back and forth above Deniliquin. After about 5 or 6 kilometres, they watched as the light transformed into a bright luminous white colour for about 5 minutes, before resuming its original configuration. (Investigator: Paul Norman/Victorian UFO Research Society; reported by Julie Grant, *Northern Times*, Kerang, Victoria, 13 November 1990)

22 November 1990: St Osyth/Clacton-on-Sea, Essex, UK
At 00.30, two security guards at a caravan site at St Osyth observed a 'boomerang-shaped' object with nine lights and a larger central light at the front edge (Figure 9:8), heading in an easterly direction towards Clacton.

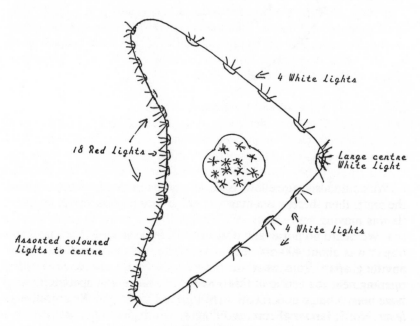

Figure 9:8.

'It had an assortment of coloured lights to its centre, and we counted eighteen red lights after it had passed us,' said one of the witnesses. 'I estimate the object to have been in excess of 250 feet [in size] . . . [and] no more than 500 feet up and about 500–600 feet from us, out over the sea. There was no noise whatsoever.'

The other witness estimated the UFO to be much larger – 400–500 feet – and at about 1,000 feet altitude. The sighting lasted for 2–3 minutes.

Two hours later, at 02.30, Mr S and Miss J were walking along the Clacton sea front when they noticed a 'triangle-shaped object' passing near the end of Clacton pier. It seemed to be slightly above the height of the pier, but no more than 50 feet or so. The object had a row of white lights along its leading edge, and the centre seemed to have more light than the sides (Figure 9:9).

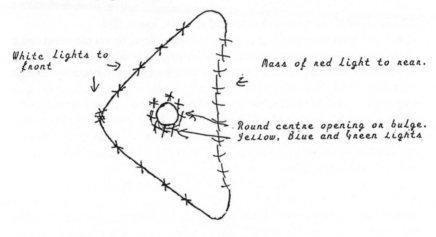

Figure 9:9.

'We could also see yellow, blue, and green lights about the centre of the craft, then there was a mass of red lights at its rear,' Mr S reported. 'It was moving very slowly. We thought it was going to crash into the sea. We heard no noise, and both felt this to be strange. The size of the object was about 400–500 feet in length . . . My girlfriend did not see anything apart from what we have stated, but I saw a large round opening near the centre of this object. If it was not an opening, it must have been a bulge underneath.' (Bill Eden, *Essex UFO Research Newsletter*, No. 5, January/February 1991)

23 November 1990: The Vumba, near Mutare, Zimbabwe
Philip, the cook of Mrs S, was sitting with his wife outside their hut when, at 22.30, they saw a very bright object suddenly appear from the south and moving north. The object was so bright that it lit up the ground for quite a way around them. There was a longish flame coming from the rear of the light, which was of a rather elongated, elliptical shape. The object was huge and noiseless, with a large light underneath and a blinking light at the front. The sighting lasted for about 5 minutes. (Kathy Newman, *UFO Afrinews*, No. 4, March 1991, edited by Cynthia Hind, P.O. Box MP 49, Mount Pleasant, Harare, Zimbabwe, Africa)

19 December 1990: Caguas, Puerto Rico
Several witnesses observed a large ball of light, pursued by military helicopters (see pp.111–112).

3 January 1991: Westhead/Bickerstaffe, Lancashire, UK
At about 19.30, Barry and Linda Dawson were driving to a motor auction on Scarth Hill when they encountered a brilliant white object in the sky. 'It was like a triangle shape, a very bright light, and it was on its own,' Barry reported. 'Cars coming the other way were slowing right down and looking . . . and there were two people walking along the road. When we came out of the auction I looked up through the windscreen and the light was there again. Three lights appeared around the bottom of it and all of a sudden it disappeared . . .' (*New Town Advertiser*, Skelmersdale, Lancashire, 10 January 1991)

6 January 1991: Liskeard, Cornwall, UK
Albert Hall, a 68-year-old Londoner living in Liskeard, was surprised by an unusual sight in the sky at about 08.00. 'The view from my lounge window is of distant fields and a broad expanse of sky,' he told the Plymouth UFO Research Group (PUFORG). 'I happened by chance to glance out of the window and witnessed the object emerging from behind the clouds . . . moving very slowly from left to right.'
   The object passed behind a cloud and Albert watched for about a minute then went to fetch his binoculars, resuming observation from another room. 'I watched the object through my binoculars for approximately 2 minutes before it disappeared behind a bank of clouds to my right . . . The object had a clearly defined outline and was brilliant white. I live in an area in which the Air Force practise low-flying exercises . . . I have also seen gas-filled balloons and, in the past, airships and barrage balloons, but this object had no wings or tailplane, or gondola attached to the underneath, and I could not see any markings or windows . . . The

140

object did not shine like a star or a planet and there was no glow . . .'

The object looked 'like a knitting needle – very slim – like a cylinder with tapered ends', and was three inches long at arms length. (Bob Boyd, Plymouth UFO Research Group Report No. 9101)

January 1991 (third week): Keckskemet, Hungary
On 21 January, Hungarian newspapers reported that the Defence Ministry was investigating a sighting the previous week of a UFO over Keckskemet military airport, south of Budapest. Officers at the airport said the object flew silently at a height of about 600 feet, trailing a 240-foot exhaust flame. 'I do not believe in UFOs,' said a military spokesman, 'but I have no reason to doubt what my fellow officers say.' (*Wall Street Journal*, New York; *Greenock Telegraph*, Scotland, 22 January 1991)

23 January 1991: Great Houghton, Yorkshire, UK
Tony Fletcher and his girlfriend Julie Creasey spotted a diamond-shaped object hovering in the sky at about 01.20. They watched for several minutes, then it suddenly started darting erratically in different directions.

'At first we thought it was an aeroplane, but it was just hovering,' said Mr Fletcher. 'It suddenly started darting all over the sky at a high speed and then went back to its original position and hovered again. We watched it for about 40 minutes and it repeated this several times. At one point it came closer, then dipped and drew away, and we could clearly see it was a diamond shape with a rounded front end: it looked something like a sting-ray. There was no noise from it, but it was sending out bright red, green and white flashing lights . . .' (*Barnsley Chronicle*, York, 25 January 1991)

22 February 1991: Leckhampstead/Maids Moreton, Buckinghamshire, UK
Returning home by car from a school reunion in a Buckinghamshire village, three youths noticed what one of them described as an object that was 'shaped unusually cigarish, fat in the middle, luminously white, glowing with [thousands of] lights radiating from all angles' at 00.45. As they reached the village of Maids Moreton at about 00.59, the object appeared closer, and seemed to flit from house to house in a jerking motion.

Parking the car in a field and switching off all lights, the witnesses continued to watch the object, now 500 yards away. At one stage, it seemed to respond by moving even closer when the driver 'signalled' to

141

it with the car headlights. At this stage, panic overcame the youths. As Jenny Randles reports:

'The object was now maybe 100 feet away on the other side of the road. [Witness] B's one thought was to get out of the field. He tried the engine and lights but both failed to respond. The ignition did not even make a sound. He tried repeatedly for about 20 seconds but to no avail. Not even the headlights functioned now. Then a brilliant beam of light poured out of the object, just 50 feet away. This enveloped the car and B could not even see the steering wheel in front of him. A faint humming sound was also reported by two of the three witnesses, but only at this point . . . C, in the front seat, tried to open the door to leap out but it was as if it were glued shut . . . One youth screamed, the others say (he denies it). A admits he lay flat on the seat, buried his head in his hands and closed his eyes.

'Reflexively, B turned the ignition again, and then everything happened at once. The light beam, humming, and UFO vanished instantly and the car was working. They drove out of the field as fast as possible the three miles into Buckingham . . .'

The witnesses reported a time lapse, but Jenny believes that there could be a rational explanation for this. The case is under investigation by BUFORA and NUFORC. (Jenny Randles, *Northern UFO News*, No. 148, April 1991)

7 March 1991: Northfield, Birmingham, UK
At 00.40 Mrs Bette Jackson became aware of an unusual noise and noticed that the area outside her cottage was illuminated. An oblong, 'Zeppelin-shaped' brightly lit object could be seen through the windows, with a beam of light extending downwards. The colour of the object was light grey.

'I then noticed that the body of the object was brightly lit through what appeared to be windows. I believe they were square . . . they appeared to be divided into three colours: one-third were white, one-third amber, and the remainder of another colour . . . The noise was a droning sound which was very penetrating and continued throughout. The object seemed to be suspended in the air . . . [The sighting] up to this point took place in about 15 minutes . . . I reached into my wardrobe where I keep my camera, a Canon EOS 750, which I keep loaded and ready to use at all times . . .

'I took three photographs through the bedroom window. I was by now very curious, and noticed at that time that someone was in the

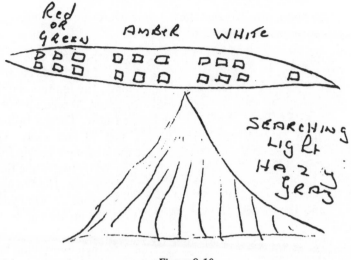

Figure 9:10.

adjoining garden [who] I believed to be my neighbour. She was standing perfectly still looking up at the same object ... I quickly rushed down the stairs, my camera still in my hand, and went outside to the rear of my cottage, and low and behold, the object was still there, suspended in the sky – beam, lights, and droning noise again. The beam appeared to be searching the area below, moving very slowly ... I took two photographs, praying that the light from the object and the beam would be sufficient ...

'After about 5 minutes, the object moved very slowly from the rear of my cottage to the front, so I went through the side gate to the front ... After another minute or two, the object returned to the rear. Of course, I followed it again, and after another 2–3 minutes the beam was switched off, then the lights went out leaving only the droning sound, which lasted I would say about another 10 seconds or so, then silence. I did not see the object move again: it simply disappeared from *my* view. I say this because I do not know what happened to it, because I saw *nothing* else ... All that I saw and heard lasted approximately 25 minutes.'

(This very interesting report was sent to me by Bette Jackson, thanks to her nephew Ron Ferrett, who informed me that the neighbour did indeed witness the same incident but fears ridicule if her name is released. Mrs Jackson also sent me the negatives of the photos she took, but unfortunately nothing at all is visible.)

143

8 March 1991: Plymouth, Devon, UK

Mary Aylesworth, an American singing teacher living in St Budeaux, Plymouth, was awakened by her cat at 05.30 – over an hour earlier than usual – and decided to feed him in case he pestered her. 'As I entered the kitchen,' she told Plymouth UFO Research Group (PUFORG) investigators, 'I looked out and saw three circular plate-like objects in the sky. Two were side by side and one was underneath the other two, in the middle. They were very close to each other – almost touching.

'They looked to be made of some kind of shiny metal, like aluminium. The thing that interested me was that each was covered by what appeared to be spotlights, as if they had been built into the surface of each of the circles. The brightness of the objects looked like normal spotlights, and the closest thing I could equate them with would be moonlight.'

All the objects maintained the same face toward the witness, even in flight, 'so I do not know what was on the other side of the "plate"'. The lights covered the faces of the objects, but none touched or overlapped the rim onto the other side. Shiny metal could be seen between the lights. The lights were flat, level with the surface of the disc, and illuminated the surface, 'shining on the metal', so the surface may have been concave.

'They seemed to be hovering . . . when I first saw them I had the feeling that they had been there some time. As I looked, the bottom one suddenly shot away to the right . . . and sort of went towards the horizon at a wide angle, as if it was going somewhere. Then about 30 seconds later, it seemed to shoot back up again and then it was underneath the "plates" . . . then another one came up and joined the group and so there were four – two plus two.

'A 50p piece [held at arm's length] would cover them individually,' said Mary, trying to estimate the size. 'It was like four 50p pieces, in other words . . . I am shortsighted and I did not have my glasses on, but I still had no trouble seeing them very clearly. The thing that struck me about them was that they moved incredibly fast . . . They kept changing position. I had a feeling they were certainly co-ordinated – the four of them together. I felt there was some kind of intelligence behind it; a logic in what they were doing . . . almost like a Red Arrows manoeuvre.'

After the first object returned to the position it had left, the formation maintained position for 2 minutes, then another object came streaking in from the left, at the same speed as the first, and took a position under the left upper object, the lower object moving to the side. They stayed in this position for approximately one and a half minutes, then the lower right object repeated its first flight and was gone. Some 10 seconds later,

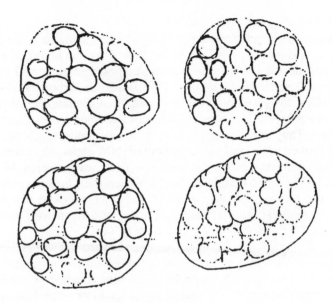

Figure 9:11.

the lower left object retraced its flight. Another 10 seconds later, the upper right object flew away, followed 10 seconds later by the last remaining one.

'Mary is an intelligent and articulate woman,' reports Bob Boyd, PUFORG's chairman. 'We found her to be a credible witness and fully accept her report as a genuine sighting of four UFOs. Thanks to articles in the [Plymouth] *Evening Herald* and *Independent*, we have received written reports from two drivers who were on the road shortly after Mary's sighting.' One of these reports follows.

Mr S was approaching Plymouth on the A38 at 06.20 when he saw, from a distance of some miles, four slightly larger than pinhead-size yellow-white stationary lights, close to a tall building in the city centre. Thinking at first that they were a flight of helicopters (a common sight in Plymouth), he realized they weren't moving and immediately slowed down the car 'to almost walking pace' and watched them for a period of 5–10 minutes while he drove along.

'Each of the lights would fade out over a period of several seconds until it disappeared completely, and after a short time would reappear,' he wrote to PUFORG. 'All four of the lights would do this from time to time, although only one at any time ... and there was no readily discernible pattern to this. Occasionally a bright flash would emanate

145

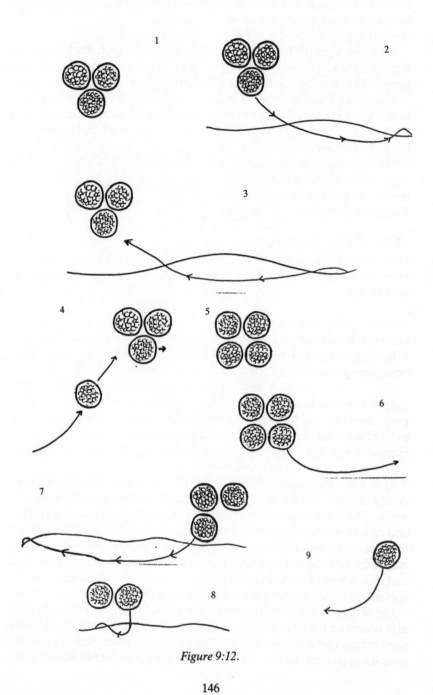

Figure 9:12.

from behind the object nearest the building, sufficiently bright to clearly illuminate the top left corner of the building, similar to a flash-gun or strobe light in intensity.'

Mr S lost sight of the objects behind trees, so he then drove out of his way into the city centre for a better look, but the objects were not seen again. The witness, with a long-standing interest in aircraft, stated 'categorically' that the objects were not 'any kind of aircraft I have ever seen', nor were they flares, balloons, Venus, or a temperature inversion. He had contacted PUFORG, he said, 'to reassure Mary that hers was not the only sighting'.

'Though the witness asked for anonymity,' Bob Boyd reports, 'he did supply us with his name, address, occupation and public position. His desire for privacy is understandable.' (Bob Boyd, PUFORG Sighting Reports Nos. 9103/4)

17 March 1991: Trujillo, Puerto Rico
Over 100 witnesses observed a large circular UFO which hovered low over the electrical substation, causing $355,000 in damage costs (see pp.112–18)

18 March 1991: Shanghai, China
For 9 minutes, an airliner chased UFOs until they headed towards the plane at high speed and disappeared above it. One of the objects was described as being larger than the British-built Shorts 360–300 (see pp.56–7).

2 April 1991: Maracaibo, Venezuela
Five glowing unidentified flying objects passed over Maracaibo, prompting a wave of calls to a local radio station. (*Portsmouth News*, Hampshire, 3 April 1991)

2 April 1991: Faribault, Minnesota, USA
At about 19.00, Dick Feichtinger had an unusual sighting while driving to work. 'I saw this object that was oblong, but it seemed to be hanging up and down. Rather than horizontal, it was vertical,' he reported, adding that the object was white, very long and narrow. Later, as he was heading home, he saw the object again, but this time it was red and green. 'The fact that it wasn't horizontal is strange – from the configuration and the way it was hanging, that was what drew my attention to it.'

On arrival home, Feichtinger summoned his wife and children, who also observed the object, confirming that it was red, green, and at times solid white, and seemed to be intelligently guided. Suddenly, low-flying aircraft appeared on the scene, also observed by other witnesses. 'I thought they were going to land on my house,' said Steve Kelly, who saw two planes flying extremely low, close to each other, and at a reduced speed. 'They were flying so low I couldn't figure out what was keeping them up there,' said Feichtinger. As he stood under a street light, he waved to the planes, and one briefly turned on what seemed to be floodlights.

Later, more aircraft (estimated by Feichtinger's son to be as many as eleven) appeared in the area. Other witnesses say they saw helicopters as well as two large airplanes. Lt Kevin Gutknecht, a spokesman for the Air National Guard, admitted that two C-130 cargo planes had been in the area and that one of the pilots turned on his landing lights. The spokesman added, however, that there were no other aircraft reported in the area, and that the two pilots did not see any strange lights in the sky. Gutknecht was equally puzzled by the report of a UFO. 'I have no idea what it is. It doesn't sound like anything we have in the Minnesota military inventory.' (Paul Adams, *Daily News*, Faribault, Minnesota, 5 April 1991)

12 April 1991: Basildon, Essex, UK
Driving home from work along the A13 road near Basildon at 19.15, Mr F. Calver noticed a large triangular dark shape (Figure 9:13) moving across the sky. As he slowed down, Mr Calver just had time to observe the object crossing the road in front of him. No noise could be heard as the UFO disappeared in the direction of Thames Haven. Duration of sighting: 2–3 seconds. (*Essex UFO Research Newsletter*, No. 7, May/June 1991, with additional details supplied by Ron West)

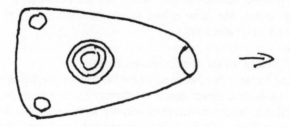

Figure 9:13.

21 April 1991: Kent, UK
Captain Achille Zaghetti, flying in an Alitalia MD-80 at 22,000 feet over Kent, reported sighting a missile, light brown in colour and 3 metres

long, flying in the opposite direction 1,000 feet above the airliner at 21.00. Simultaneously, a faint radar image was detected 10 miles behind the plane on radar at London Air Traffic Control Centre, West Drayton.

Duncan Lennox, editor of *Jane's Strategic Weapons*, said the description fitted that of a target missile or drone used for air defence practice, which are typically 3.5 metres long, turbojet powered, and fly at a speed of 400 m.p.h. This would seem to be the explanation, since the incident occurred almost directly above Lydd Ranges, a Ministry of Defence firing range in Kent. The MoD, however, denied that any such missiles or drones were in use on 21 April. 'Whatever [the pilot] might have seen', said a spokesman, 'might have been something that was flying, but was certainly not anything that was fired. It was a Sunday. The only ranges we have in the Kent area are Lydd and Hythe, and they are concerned with small arms only.'

The spokesman added that remotely piloted vehicles (RPVs) were sometimes used as targets for test firings, but they never went to 22,000 feet. 'It's absolutely in the middle of the busiest traffic area,' he said. 'People don't just fire missiles there, but of course, we do have quite a few UFO reports and often people who see these things describe them as missile- or cigar-shaped, or else round, and sometimes they do appear to be travelling with no means of propulsion.' (*The Sunday Times*, London, 5 May 1991/Stephen Ward, *The Independent/The Times*, London, 6 May 1991)

30 April 1991: Walton-on-the-Naze, Essex, UK
Three witnesses, walking along the sea front at 20.35, noticed a large oblong object, the size of two double-decker buses, with two sets of yellow lighted 'windows or portholes' along its side (Figure 9:14), out over the sea, moving from east to west. The object was estimated to be about 750 feet away, at an altitude of approximately 500 feet. No sound could be heard. It appeared to be hovering, then would move off at speed, stop, and hover again. It then returned to its original position, hovered for about 5 minutes, finally shooting off at speed towards Frinton-on-Sea. (*Essex UFO Research Newsletter*, No. 7, May/June 1991)

(It is worth comparing this description and sketch with the report of a black object with two sets of lighted 'windows', alleged to have been seen at Benfleet, Essex, on 30 January 1989, published in *The UFO Report 1991*, p.215.)

Figure 9:14.

3/4 May 1991: Southend-on-Sea, Essex, UK
Two security men, Mr T and Mr W, were driving along the seafront at
Southend at 23.39 when they noticed an oval-shaped orange light out to
sea which seemed to be keeping pace with them. They stopped the car
for a better view, and the light stopped too. It seemed to be close to the
Kent side of the Thames Estuary. The oval orange light appeared to
have a glow around it (Figure 9:15). The witnesses also thought they
could see other lights within the orange light, but could not be certain of
this. They watched for about 5 minutes as the object remained hovering.

Figure 9:15.

The security men had to check a building further down the road, so
decided to drive on. The oval light again appeared to be following them,
and on each occasion that they stopped and started, the light did
likewise. On reaching the building, the men parked, with the light
hovering in the distance. Ten minutes later, when they had completed
their check, the men returned to their vehicle to find that the object had
vanished.

Later that night, the same (or similar) object was seen in the vicinity
by two other security men. At 02.30, having finished their shift and
driving home between Benfleet and Canvey Island, Essex, the witnesses
were forced to make an emergency stop when a very large oval orange

light shot across their field of view. The object was surrounded by a glow and seemed to be about 200 feet long and 50 feet wide. Coloured lights could be seen within the main orange glow. The silent object was estimated to be at an altitude of approximately 1,000 feet, an elevation of 45 degrees, and about a mile away. After 2–3 minutes, the object disappeared in the direction of Southend. (*Essex UFO Research Newsletter*, No. 7, May/June 1991)

17 May 1991: Sichuan Province, China
The crew of a Boeing 707 airliner was obliged to take evasive action following a close approach by a large, round object, at about 22.00. The UFO was also observed by the crew of another airliner (see p.57).

18 May 1991: St Osyth, Essex, UK
Three men fishing near St Osyth suddenly heard a buzzing sound at 00.30, followed by the sight of an object with lighted 'windows' in the sky. It appeared as if 'people' were looking out of the windows (Figure 9:16). Just as suddenly as it appeared, the object disappeared. (*Essex UFO Research Newsletter*, No. 7, May/June 1991)

Figure 9:16.

22/3 May 1991: Nottingham, UK
Numerous witnesses in the Nottingham area reported sightings of low-flying, brightly illuminated UFOs between 23.40 and 00.40. Mrs Elaine Buck of Gedling saw two lights resembling elongated triangles, making a faint humming sound. 'The lights were very bright, almost like Concorde in shape, but rounded at the end,' said Mrs Buck. 'There were also red and green lights but the white ones were brilliant and lit up all the underneath.'

Fifteen minutes later Jack and Mavis Sargent saw the same phenomenon as they were driving home in Arnold. 'There were two diamond-shaped lights, about 1,000 feet up,' said Mr Sargent. 'I ran into the house [on arrival home] and got my binoculars, then I could see they were no more than a few feet apart. There was a low, humming or pumping noise . . . Each object was about six times bigger than any aircraft, I know.' Mr Sargent rang his son in Arnold, and he and his wife also saw the objects.

Derek Winfield of Ilkeston was the last to report a sighting, at about 00.20, which lasted for 20 minutes. He was at work at Heanor Gate Industrial Estate when a workmate called him. They ran into the yard where they saw two big lights. His colleague shouted and waved at the objects as they came towards them. There, they stopped for a minute. 'We must have been visible due to the floodlights,' said Mr Winfield. 'We got the impression that it was observing us.'

Reports also came in to the East Midlands UFO Research Association and Quest International from witnesses in Beeston, Bestwood, Calverton, Kimberley and Heanor. (Lynette Tasker, *Nottingham, Evening Post*, 24 May/4 June 1991)

5 June 1991: Clacton-on-Sea, Essex, UK
Just after midnight, Mrs P was on her way home, having just left a friend's house. Walking down the street, she glanced up at the sky and saw a glowing orange ball of light, surrounded by a paler orange halo, moving from west to east along the sea front. She watched for at least 10 minutes as the ball moved to and fro and up and down, without any sound, below the cloud base. The object then suddenly shot straight up into the clouds and disappeared. For approximately a minute, the clouds retained an orange tint where the object had entered. (Essex UFO Research Group)

27 June 1991: Near Colchester, Essex, UK
Two witnesses were driving along the B1022 from Tiptree towards Colchester when they encountered an unusual sight. 'My wife and I saw a large, square-shaped object about 200 feet above a field on our right, approximately two fields away from us. It had two blue and two red lights, and was moving in the direction of Mersea Island. No noise was heard . . .' (Essex UFO Research Group)

Appendix

Some UFO Organizations

(Australia, Canada, UK and USA)

Australia

Australian Centre for UFO Studies, P.O. Box 728, Lane Cove, NSW 2066.

UFO Research Australia, P.O. Box 229, Prospect, South Australia 5082.

UFO Research Queensland, P.O. Box 111, North Quay, Queensland 4002.

Victorian UFO Research Society, P.O. Box 43, Moorabbin, Victoria 3189.

Canada

Canadian UFO Research Network, P.O. Box 15, Station 'A', Willowdale, Ontario, M2N 5S7.

Centrale de Compilation Ufologique de Quebec, CP 103, Drummondville, Quebec, J2B 2V6.

UFO Research Institute of Canada, Depart. 25, 1665 Robson Street, Vancouver, British Columbia, V6G 3C2.

Ufology Research of Manitoba, P.O. Box 1918, Winnipeg, Manitoba, 3RC 3R2.

United Kingdom

British UFO Research Association, 16 Southway, Burgess Hill, Sussex, RH15 9ST.

Contact International (UK), 11 Ouseley Close, New Marston, Oxford, OX3 0JS.

Essex UFO Research Group, 95 Chilburn Road, Great Clacton, Essex, CO15 4PE.

Plymouth UFO Research Group, 40 Albert Road, Stoke, Plymouth, PL2 1AE.

Scottish Research into UFOs, 129 Langton View, East Calder, West Lothian, EH53 0RE.

Surrey Investigation Group on Aerial Phenomena, Durfold Lodge, Plaistow Road, Dunsfold, Surrey, GU8 4PQ.

Quest International, 18 Hardy Meadows, Grassington, Skipton, North Yorkshire, BD23 5DL.

United States of America

Citizens Against UFO Secrecy, 3518 Martha Custis Avenue, Alexandria, Virginia 22302.

J. Allen Hynek Center for UFO Studies, 2457 W. Peterson Avenue, Chicago, Illinois 60659.

Fund for UFO Research, P.O. Box 277, Mount Rainier, Maryland 20712.

Mutual UFO Network, 103 Oldtowne Road, Seguin, Texas 78155–4099.

UFO Reporting & Information Service, P.O. Box 832, Mercer Island, Washington 98040.

Pennsylvania Association for the Study of the Unexplained, 6 Oak Hill Avenue, Greensburg, Pennsylvania 15601.

The Crop Circles

Centre for Crop Circle Studies

The CCCS was founded in 1990, with Professor Archie Roy, BSc., PhD., FRAS, as President. The main objective of CCCS is to conduct well organized research into the phenomena of Crop Circles and pictograms, both in the UK and overseas, and to publish its data and findings in CCCS publications and other serious outlets. CCCS is very conscious of the fact that the Crop Circles occur almost invariably on private land owned or cultivated by the farming community, and encourages its members and affiliates to adhere to a strict Code of Practice, agreement on which has been reached with the National Farmers' Union.

For further details, send a stamped addressed envelope (UK only) to: CCCS, c/o SKS, 20 Paul Street, Frome, Somerset, BA11 1DX.

Some UFO Journals

Flying Saucer Review

Edited by Gordon Creighton, MA, FRGS, FRAS, with an international team of consultants, *FSR* is arguably the leading journal on the subject of UFOs and is taken by many governmental bodies and institutions, including the Chinese Institute of Scientific & Technical Information and the USSR Academy of Sciences.

For subscription details, send a stamped addressed envelope to: The Editor, FSR Publications Ltd, P.O. Box 162, High Wycombe, Buckinghamshire, HP13 5DZ, UK.

Fortean Times

A quarterly journal devoted to news, notes, reviews, and references on all manner of strange phenomena, continuing the work of Charles Fort (1874–1932). Write to: *Fortean Times*, SKS, 20 Paul Street, Frome, Somerset, BA11 1DX. (Now widely available.)

International UFO Reporter

Published by the J. Allen Hynek Center for UFO Studies, *IUR* is one of the two leading UFO journals in the USA. Address enquiries to: *International UFO Reporter*, 2457 W. Peterson Avenue, Chicago, Illinois 60659, USA.

Journal of UFO Research
A bi-monthly Chinese-language journal with the world's largest circulation, devoted to UFOs and science. Write for details to: Paul Dong, P.O. Box 2011, Oakland, California 94604, USA.

Just Cause
Edited by Barry Greenwood and published by Lawrence Fawcett (authors of *Clear Intent*), this journal is essential reading for those interested in the US Government cover-up. Write to: CAUS, P.O. Box 218, Coventry, Connecticut 06238, USA.

MUFON UFO Journal
Published by the Mutual UFO Network (the world's leading UFO organization) with a staff of reporters and columinists second to none, the *MUFON UFO Journal* has established itself as one of the finest magazines on the subject in the world. Write to: MUFON, 103 Oldtowne Road, Seguin, Texas 78155–4099, USA.

Northern UFO News
Edited by Jenny Randles, this journal is always packed with fascinating reports that are seldom published elsewhere. Write to: NUFON, 37 Heathbank Road, Cheadle Heath, Stockport, Cheshire, SK3 OUP, UK.

Quest International: The Journal of UFO Investigation
Edited by Graham Birdsall, *Quest International* is a popular journal featuring articles by a wide variety of international contributors. Official documents, slides, audio and video tapes, etc., are also available from this organization.

Send a large stamped addressed envelope to Quest Publications International Ltd, 15 Pickard Court, Temple Newsam, Leeds, Yorkshire, LS15 9AY, UK.

Services

Books on UFOs
Those requiring books on UFOs which are not currently available in bookshops should write, enclosing a large stamped addressed envelope, to: Susanne Stebbing, 41 Terminus Drive, Herne Bay, Kent, CT6 6PR, UK, or Arcturus Book Service, P.O. Box 831383, Stone Mountain, Georgia 30083–0023, USA.

UFO Newsclipping Service
The UFO Newsclipping Service will keep you informed of all the latest United States and worldwide reports, many of which are carried only in local newspapers.
For subscription details, write to: Lucius Farish, UFO Newsclipping Service, Route 1, Box 220, Plumerville, Arkansas 72127, USA.

UK Newsclippings
For those requiring UK newsclippings only, a service is provided by CETI Publications in association with Quest Publications International Ltd. For subscription details, send a 22×11cm. stamped addressed envelope to: CETI, 247 High Street, Beckenham, Kent, BR3 1AB, UK.

UFO Call
The British UFO Research Association and British Telecom run a 24-hour UFO news update service on (0898) 121886.

UFO Hotline
Quest International has a 24-hour UFO Hotline for reporting sightings in the UK. Telephone (0756) 752216.

Computer UFO Network/UFO Reporting & Information Service
CUFON was established in the USA by Dale Goudie for the purpose of providing other researchers with quick access to sighting data and locations, as well as documented Freedom of Information material.   Connect at 300 or 1200 bauds, eight data bits, no parity, one stop bit: USA (206) 721 5035, from 20.00 – 08.00 hrs. WST. The UFO Reporting & Information Service functions from 08.00 – 20.00 hrs.

MUFON Amateur Radio Net
   80 metres – 3.990 MHz, Saturdays, 22.00 hrs.
   40 metres – 7.237 MHz, Saturdays, 08.00 hrs.
   10 metres – 28.460 MHz. Thursdays, 20.00 hrs.
   10 metres – 28.470 MHz. Sundays, 15.00 hrs.
All times are Eastern Standard or Daylight.

Reporting Sightings

The majority of UFO sightings turn out to have a mundane explanation, such as aircraft, aircraft landing lights, balloons, meteors (shooting stars), laser shows, planets, re-entry of terrestrial space hardware (including satellites, which can also look impressive when orbiting), stars, etc., but if you *really* think you may have seen something exotic, do contact one or more of the organizations listed above. In addition, the police will investigate a sighting if it is considered sufficiently important, and they are required to submit a report to the Ministry of Defence, as are military bases and air traffic control officers (in the UK), but in most instances the report is simply filed away and neglected. The MoD takes UFO reports seriously and will be glad to note down all the details if you approach them directly but, unless specifically requested, seldom notify witnesses of their findings.

If your sighting was particularly impressive (*not* just an odd light in the sky), I recommend that you contact the newsdesk of a national newspaper, in order that we may all learn about it with the minimum delay – assuming the editor decides to run the story. Also, an appeal for any additional witnesses should be made via your local newspaper, radio and/or TV station.

The 1992 Yearbook of Astronomy

For amateur astronomers and ufologists alike, the *Yearbook* (edited by Patrick Moore and published by Sidgwick & Jackson) is an invaluable guide to the night sky, and contains a variety of articles by major contributors from the international community of astronomers, as well as star charts for both northern and southern hemisphere observers, backed up by useful information lists on planets, comets, meteors, eclipses, stars, etc.

Index

ABC TV, 98
Abductions, 70–71, 82
Acosta, Dolin, 110
Acosta, Roosevelt, 110
Adams, Paul, 148
Adorno, José, 116
Adorno, Sonia, 116
Aeroplane & Armament
    Experimental Establishment
    (MoD), 126
Aerospace Knowledge, 57
Ai, Xianfu, 52
Air Traffic Control Agency (China),
    55, 56
Akitaev, Emil, 69
Alitalia, 148–9
Andrews, Colin, 5–6, 7–8, 9, 10, 11,
    13, 28
Andrews, Richard, 2, 11
Army Weather Bureau (China), 55
Artem, Mashmich, 67
Ashley, Edith, 37
Atomic Energy Commission, 39
Authority of Electrical Energy
    (Puerto Rico), 117–18
AWACS, 102–3
Aylesworth, Mary, 144–7

Bachurin, Emil, 77
Baoshan TV station, 54
Barron, Joe, 123
Bauer, Roy, 22
Bauerlein, Richard, 133
BBC TV, 6–7, 9, 13
Begaliev, Dr S., 70

Belgian Air Force, vii
Benítez, Rafael, 114
Bentley, John, 122
Beshmetov, P. , 76
Biesele, Mildred, 130
Bigas, Genaro, 115
'Bigfoot', 69–70
Birdsall, Graham, 155
Blazhis, Cpl A., 74, 76
Boyd, Bob, 130–1, 141, 145–7
Bozhich, Dr Sergei, 59
Bratton Castle, 8
British Airways (sightings), viii, 126,
    136
British Army, 6, 8, 9, 12, 13, 14
Broadhurst, Paul, 15
Broom, Kelly, 134–5
Buck, Elaine, 151
BUFORA, 142, 156
Bulantsev, Sergei, 60, 62
Butt, Bill, 11

Cabo Rojo (Puerto Rico), viii
Calver, F., 148
Cameron, Grant, 22, 28, 33, 34, 36,
    37
Carson, Tim, 5
Cauti, Jimmy, 10
Center for UFO Studies, 105
Central Intelligence Agency (CIA),
    39, 46–7, 79
Centre for Crop Circle Studies
    (CCCS), 1, 15, 154
Chernouss, Dr Sergei, 59
Chinese Institute of Scientific &

Technical Information, 154
Chorost, Michael, 28
Churchill, Sir Winston, 40
Colonel 'X' (USSR), 77
Collado, Benito, 106, 109
Committee for the Scientific
  Investigation of Claims of the
  Paranormal (CSICOP), 28, 29
Cook, Duane, 83, 93
Cosmic Journey Project, ix–x
Cosmic rays, 79
Creasey, Julie, 141
Creighton, Gordon, 154
Cropfield Circles (UK only):
  Alton Barnes, 4–6, 12, 14
  Army involvement, 6, 8, 9, 12, 13,
  14
  Barbury Castle, 18, 19, 20
  Beckhampton, 14, 18–19
  Bickington, 15
  Bratton Castle, 8
  Bratton hoax, 7–12, 13, 14, 16
  Butleigh, 16–17
  Celtic Cross, 2
  Cheesefoot Head, 2, 3, 14–15
  Chilcomb, 2
  Devizes, 2
  dowsing, 15, 17, 19–20, 28
  dumb-bell shapes, 1, 3, 4, 5
  Duns, 15
  East Field, 5
  East Kennett, 14
  Gt Yarmouth, 126
  hoaxes, 7–12, 13, 14, 16, 17, 20–21,
  29
  Hopton, 15
  'Horoscope' game, 7, 10, 12, 13
  ley lines, 20
  Litchfield, 3
  luminous phenomena, 3–4, 15–16,
  18–19, 36
  Margate, 20–21
  'Mary current', 15, 16
  Milk Hill, 4, 5–6
  noises, 3, 5, 16
  North Walsham, 127
  Operation Blackbird, 6, 7, 8, 9, 10,
  13, 14
  Pepperbox Hill, 15
  pictograms, 3, 4–5, 12, 14, 15, 16,

  18, 19, 28, 29, 34, 35
  'Plasma vortex', 17, 18, 28
  Preshute Farm, 19
  Project White Crow, 6
  rewards, 14, 29
  Silbury Hill, 3, 15
  Swafield, 15
  symbols, 5, 20, 34
  UFOs, 5–6, 7, 15, 16–17, 18–19,
  26–29
  video film, 5–6, 7
  Wandlebury, 15
  Wansdyke, 3–4
  Wigan, 15
  Wootton Bassett, 19
Cummings, Cpl Darren, 8, 13
Cybulski, Flt Lt M., 41

D'Alton, Capt. Mike, 136
Dane, David, 126, 127
Daugherty, Roy, 128–9
Dávila, Rose, 100–1
Dawson, Barry, 140
Dawson, Linda, 140
Day, Fred, 14
Dean, Robert, x
De Brouwer, Col Wilfried, vii
Deetkin, Chad, 34, 35, 36
Defense Intelligence Agency (DIA),
  39
Delgado, Pat, 6, 7, 9, 10, 13, 17, 28
De Trafford, George, 15, 17
Dewis, Sgt, 41
Díaz, Ramses, 116
Diodonet, Luis, 109–10
Dmitreiv, Dr Aleksei, 61
Dodd, Tony, 133, 134, 135
Dolotov, Aleksandr, 70–1
Dolotov, Dr Rita, 70–1
Dolphin, Flt Lt, 40
Druffel, Ann, ix
Drummond, Bill, 10
Dudnik, Cpl S., 75–6
Duplin, Maj. A. L., 73–4

East Midlands UFO Research
  Association, 152
Eden, Bill, 139
Edwards, Sqdn Ldr G. D., 45
Eltsin, M. S., 66, 68

Electrical effects (power cuts & fluctuations), 66, 112–18, 127, 142
Estonian Commission on Anomalous Phenomena, 65

F-14 Tomcat, 101–2
F-18 Hornet, 104
Farish, Lucius, 33, 37, 155
Fawcett, George, 136
Fawcett, Lawrence, 155
Federal Aviation Administration (FAA), 133
Federal Bureau of Investigation (FBI), 39
Feichtinger, Dick, 147–8
Ferrett, Ron, 143
Figueroa, Miguel, 106–9
Feschin, Dr V., 59
Filer, Maj. George, 82
Flannigan, Charles, 94
Fletcher, Tony, 141
Flynn, Carla, 121
Fort, Charles, 154
Freedon of Information Act (FOIA), 39, 40, 42
Frola, Phillip, 122, 125, 128
Fuller, John, ix
Fuller, Paul, 28
Fund for UFO Research, 81, 82, 154

García, José Luis, 117
Gardner, John, 84
Glitter, Gary, 10
Goddard Space Flight Center (NASA), 80, 81, 84, 85
Gomez, Wilfred, 21
Gorbachev, President Mikhail, vii, 64
Gordon, Stan, 33, 35
Goriacheva, Dr Olga, 71
Gorin, Sgt B., 74
Grant, Julie, 138
Green, Amanda, 125
Greenwood, Barry, 155
Grimes, Leading Aircraftsman, 41
Grist, Brian, 18–19
Gulf Breeze (Florida):
  abductions, 82, 87, 97
  circles, 97–8

Government interest, 93
High School, 84, 97–8
Joint Chiefs of Staff meeting, 93
landing traces, 97–8
mail interference, 93
missing time, 94
Nimslo camera, 85
photographic evidence, 83–5, 87–9, 90–92, 96–7
Pensacola Naval Air Station, 93, 95
Players Golf & Country Club, 93
Polaroid film analysis, 87–9
PSE tests, 83
sightings, 81, 85, 87, 94–6, 97
SRS camera, 85, 96
UFO model, 89
video film analysis, 85–6
Gutknecht, Lt Kevin, 148

Haddenham, Denise, 129–30
Haddenham, Stephen, 129–30
Haddington, Lord, 3
Haines, Dr Richard, 81
Hall, Albert, 140–1
Hardwick, Gary, 18
Harland, Jeff, 22, 37
Harrington, Michael, viii
Harris, Dave, 16, 17
Harris, Paul, 21
Hay, John, 127–8
Hi, Jiyun, 50–51
Hill-Norton, Adml Lord, viii
Hind, Cynthia, 140
Hongqaio Airport, 55, 56
Hough, Peter, 121, 124
Hungarian Defence Ministry, 141
Hynek, Dr J. Allen, 106
Hypnotic regression, 62, 92

Idaho National Guard, 34
Inman, Adm. B. R., x
Isakov, T. A., 68

Jackson, Bette, 142–3
JAMMs/KLF (pop group), 10–11
Japan Air Lines, 55
Jin, Xing, 56
Johnson, Don, 36
Journal of Meteorology, 21
Joint Chiefs of Staff, 93

Kai, Guohua, 51
Kalugin, K. P., 68
Kapov, E., 65
Kazak, V. P., 67
Kelly, Steve, 148
Kilburn, Flt Lt John, 40–41
King, Jonathan, 9
Kingston, Isabelle, 4
Klepikov, Dr V., 59
Knaup, T. M., 67
Knowles, Nick, 20–21
Kopetko, Deriece, 137–8
Kuczera, Simon, 126
Kulikova, Dr G., 59
Kuzmin, Vladimir, 61–2
Kuzofkin, Dr, 61

L-29 Akrobat, 63
L-29 Delfin, 63
Laguna Cartegena (Puerto Rico), 108, 109
Larregoity, Zahíra, 112
Lazarevich, Leonid, 72–3
Lazeiko, Capt. P., 74
Lennox, Duncan, 149
Liang, Yingxiong, 52
Limbo, Harry, 84
Litwin, Wallace, 42
London Air Traffic Control Centre, 149
Lozada, Orlando, 117
Lu, Chenming, 54

Maccabee, Dr Bruce, 79, 81, 84, 96
McNeff, Bill, 133
Magnetic fluctuations, 61
Mail on Sunday, 14
Makashov, Gen., 77
Maltsev, Gen. Igor, vii, 78
Manakov, G. M., 72–3
Manakulov, Dr M., 69–70
Manning-Philips, Jane, 126
Marrero, Josué, 113
Mathews, Gordon, 22
Meaden, Dr G. Terence, 18, 21, 28
Mei, Qi, 49–50
Meldrum, Debbie, 123–4
Meteors, 137, 156
Michaud, Ruth, 125
Migulin, Dr V., 59, 61

Miketenok, Sgt, 73
Miliaev, Dr Valeri, 59
Miller, Hamish, 15, 17
Millington, Simon, 21
Ministry of Defence (MoD):
    Deputy Directorate of Intelligence, 43–5, 47
    Directorate of Scientific Intelligence, 42, 45–6
    Misc. references, 12, 13, 39–40, 42, 45, 46, 47–8, 126, 149, 156
Miranda, José, 113
Missing time, 76, 94
Monroe, Burt, 135
Moore, P., 156
Moroz, O., 78
MUFON, 34, 36, 37, 80, 81, 82, 94, 96–7

NASA, 58, 81, 84, 85
National Air Guard (Puerto Rico), 104, 111, 112
National Caribbean Rain Forest, 99
National Security Agency (NSA), 39
National Space Council, ix–x
National Weather Service (Puerto Rico), 116, 118
NATO, x, 41, 42
Neate, Alan, 135
Neate, David, 135
Newman, Kathy, 140
Nilsson, Walter, 22
Nippon TV, 6, 98
Norman, Marion, 135
Norman, Paul, 138
North American Institute for Crop Circle Research (NAICCR), 22, 38
Novosibirsk State University, 60–1

Oechsler, Bob, ix, x
Office of the President of the US, 93
Omega Studios (Rockville, Md.), 84
Operation Blackbird, 6–10, 13, 14
Operation Mainbrace (NATO), 42, 43, 46, 47
Overlade, Dr Dan, 83
Ozone layer, 78

Panfilovski Hospital (USSR), 70
Panov, Dr Alexander, 59

Paris, Flt Officer R. N., 41
Pavlov, E., 64–5
Pensacola Naval Air Station, 93, 95
Perez, José, 106
Phillips, Miles, 37
Phillips, Ted, 26, 27–8, 29, 38
Physical effects, 61, 66, 67, 70–1
Physical traces, 22–3, 24–5, 26, 27, 30, 67, 69, 97–8
Pierce, Todd, 121
Platov, Dr Yulii, 59
Polaroid Corporation, 84, 85
Police (UK), 125, 133, 156
Pratt, Bob, 106
Pringle, Lucy, 15
Proetski, Dr, 61
Project White Crow, 6
Prokoshin, S., 72
Psychological Stress Evaluation (PSE), 83
Public Record Office (PRO), 42, 45–6, 48
Putuo District Education Institute (China), 54

Quest International, 152, 154, 155

Radar cases, 43, 44–5, 72, 73–7, 79, 133, 149
Randles, Jenny, 28, 121, 124, 142, 155
Read, David, 5, 11, 14
Remotely Piloted Vehicles (RPVs), 6, 14, 149
Riabishev, Maj. P., 72
Rizzo, Enzo, 116–17
Rodríguez, Danny, 115
Rodríguez, José, 103
Rodríguez, Luis, 116
Rodríguez, Mario, 111–12
Rogo, D. Scott, ix
Romanov, Sgt A., 74, 76
Roosevelt Roads Naval Station (Puerto Rico), 100, 101, 103, 104, 112, 119
Roswell (New Mexico) crash, 105
Royal Air Force (RAF):
  Coltishall, 43
  Dishforth, 41
  Germany, 136–7

Fighter Command HQ, 44–5
  Neatishead, 43, 44, 46, 47
  Topcliffe, 40–42, 43, 45, 46, 47
  Misc. references, 135, 136–7, 140
Royal Canadian Mounted Police (RCMP), 33
Rubtsov, Dr Vladimir, 59, 62
Rudzit, Capt. D., 74, 76, 77
Russell, Flt Lt C. P. B., 44
Rutkowski, Chris, 22

Sadovskaia, Ludmila, 67
Salter, John, 33, 36
Savoschin, S. I., 68
Sargent, Jack, 151
Sargent, Mavis, 151
Satellites, 137, 156
Scobelev, B. Y., 60
Shanghai Association for UFO Research, 54
Shanghai Radio, 54
Shapiro, Rear Adm. S., x
Sheppard, Capt. Graham, viii
Sidelnikov, Capt. A., 69
Silbury Hill, 3, 6
Simosko, Vladimir, 22
Sitnik, A. L., 67
Skyquakes, 97, 136
Smith, Emily, 136
Smith, Tommy, Jr, 90–92
Sokolov, Dr V., 59
Solloway, Alan, 126
Song, Liang, 51–3
Sosa, Wilson, 106, 109
Soviet Air Force/Air Defence Forces, vii, 72, 74, 77–79
Soviet Defence Ministry, 76, 77–9
Stafford, Irena, 135–6
Stanford, Ray, 80–1
Stewart, Rachael, 134–5
Strainic, Michael, 36, 37
Stratton, Group Capt. J. A., 41
Strekalov, G. M., 72–3
Stump, Vice Adm. Felix, 42
Suárez, Evelyn, 115–16
Sunday Sport, 12
Sunday Telegraph, vii
Swamp gas, 4

Tarr, Richard, 135

Tasker, Lynette, 152
Taylor, Busty, 11
Thompson, Master Sgt, 41
Timmerman, John, 105
Torres, Elizabeth, 116
Tretiak, Gen. Ivan, vii, 77–9
Trevisan, Janet, 15
TV South (TVS), 20–21

UFO reports:
 Alitalia, 148
 Babinda, Qld (Australia), 128
 Barham, Victoria (Australia), 137–8
 Basildon, Essex (UK), 148
 Belgium, vii, 137
 Benfleet, Essex (UK), 149
 Bickington, Devon (UK), 15
 Boscombe Down, Wilts. (UK), 126
 Brisbane, Qld (Australia), 125
 Bristol (UK), 133, 134–5
 British Airways, viii, 136
 Butleigh, Somerset (UK), 16–17
 Cabo Rojo (PR), 99
 Caguas (PR), 111–12
 Chelabinsk (USSR), 61–2
 China (misc.), 50–51
 Clacton, Essex (UK), 131, 138–9,
  152
 Dnepropetrovsk (USSR), 60
 Earth orbit, 72–3
 El Yunque (PR), 99–101
 Faribault, Minnesota (US), 147–8
 Ft Allen (PR), 103–5
 France, 137
 Frunze (USSR), 65–7, 68–9
 Genoa (Italy), 136
 Germany, 136–7
 Gloucester (UK), 135
 Gt Houghton, Yorks (UK), 141
 Gt Yarmouth, Norfolk (UK), 126
 Grozniy, Georgia (USSR), 72
 Guavate (PR), 101–3
 Gulf Breeze, Fla. (US), 94–7
 Hopton, Norfolk (UK), 15
 Hoyt Lakes, Minn. (US), 321–3
 Huangshi, Hubei (China), 49–50
 Ji Yong, Sichuan (China), 57
 Kazachstan (USSR), 60
 Keckskemet (Hungary), 141
 Kent (UK), 148–9

Kingston-upon-Hull, Humberside
 (UK), 125
Kirkenes (Norway), 47
Kirwan, Qld (Australia), 122
Kohtla-Iarve, Estonia (USSR),
 64–5
Kolskii Peninsula (USSR), 60
Leckhampstead, Bucks. (UK),
 141–2
Liskeard, Cornwall (UK), 140–1
Louisville, Kentucky (US), 135
Luton, Beds. (UK), 130–1
Manchester, N.H. (US), 125
Maracaibo (Venezuela), 147
Mount Airy, N.C. (US), 135
Murmansk (USSR), 129
Mutare (Zimbabwe), 140
North Sea, 136
Northfield, Birmingham (UK),
 142–3
North Huntingdon, Penn. (US),
 122
Nottingham (UK), 151–2
Odessa (USSR), 60
Operation Mainbrace (NATO),
 42, 47
Oktoberskaya (USSR), 62
Oliveras (PR), 109–10
Pensacola, Fla. (US), 96–7, 123
Pewsey Down, Wilts. (UK), 5–6
Plymouth, Devon (UK), 144–7
Point Clear, Essex (UK), 131–2
RAF Germany, 136–7
Runcorn, Cheshire (UK), 120
Saddleworth Moor, Lancs. (UK),
 133
St Mary's Loch, Selkirk (UK),
 127–8
St Osyth, Essex (UK), 138–9, 151
Samara (USSR), 73–7
Shanghai (China), 53–7
Sichuan Province (China), 51–2, 57
Sihong City, Jiangsu (China),
 50–51
Southend, Essex (UK), 150
Switzerland, 137
Tbilisi, Georgia (USSR), 72
Thanet, Kent (UK), 134
Topcliffe, Yorkshire (UK), 40–42
Trujillo Alto (PR), viii, 112–18

Turin (Italy), 137
Tversk (USSR), 60
Ukraine (USSR), 60
Uxbridge, Middx (UK), 135
Uzbekistan (USSR), 60
Walton, Essex (UK), 149
Warrior, Alabama (US), 121
Westhead, Lancs. (UK), 140
West Jordan, Utah (US), 129–30
Widnes, Cheshire (UK), 121
Williams Lake, B.C. (Canada),
 123–4
Workington, Cumbria (UK), 128–9
Wymondham, Norfolk (UK), 124
Xiangcheng, Sichuan (China), 57
Yabucoa (PR), 103
Yalta (USSR), 60
UFO entities:
Cabo Rojo (PR), 105–9
Gulf Breeze, Florida (US), 87
Kairma, Frunze (USSR), 65–8
Leningrad (USSR), 70–1
UFO Research of Manitoba
 (UFOROM), 22, 33–7, 38, 153
UK Government, 12, 13, 39, 40, 41,
 47, 48
Ultraviolet radiation, 63
UNITAS, 104
US Air Force, 80
US Army, 103–5
US Government, 39, 93, 119
US House of Representatives, 93
US Intelligence Community, 80
US Navy, 93, 99, 101, 104
US Postal Service, 93
US Senate, ix, 93
USS Franklin D. Roosevelt, 42
University of Maryland, 80
Ursul, A. D., 62
USSR Academy of Sciences, 59, 63,
154

Valdés, José, 101–2, 112
Valdés, Matilde, 101–2
Vandenberg, Richard, 84
Varenitsa, A., 74, 76
Velasco, Jean-Jaques, 137
Vernon, George, 11–12
Vityaev, Evgenii, 60
Volodarski Hospital (Leningrad),
 70, 71
Vorozhtsov, Evgenii, 60

Walters, Ed, 82, 83, 85, 87, 88, 89,
 90, 92–3, 94, 95–6, 97–8
Walters, Frances, 82, 83, 87, 89
Ward, Stephen, 149
Weibe, Edward, 84
West, Ron, 148
Westcott, Guy, 28
Whitehead, Paul, 136
White House, ix–x, 5
Willis, Wayne, 122
Winfield, Derek, 152
Wintle, Richard, 18
Witchell, Nicholas, 7
Woolaway, Peter, ix
Wright, Dan, 121, 122, 123, 125,
 133, 135

Xie, Dr Chu, 57

Yang, Xuan, 52–3

Zaghetti, Capt. Achille, 148–9
Zhao, Gang, 53–4
Zhibizov, Dr Svengenii, 61
Zhu, Capt., 56–7
Zhuravliev, Dr Victor, 61
Zigel, Dr Felix, 59–60, 61